Dec

Time

you   e

Anna

GET VISIBLE

HOW TO HAVE MORE IMPACT, INFLUENCE AND INCOME

ANNA PARKER-NAPLES

Get Visible
How to Have More Impact Influence and Income.
Second Edition.

Copyright © Anna Parker-Naples (2019, 2021)

ISBN13: 978-1-9163069-2-9

Published by Jumping Lion Publications

Requests to publish work from this book should be sent to:
anna@annaparkernaples.com

CONTENTS

PRAISE FOR GET VISIBLE

"To be successful in business, first you need to get noticed. This book teaches you how to become visible, credible & scalable in your field."

ROB MOORE - MULTIPLE BESTSELLING AUTHOR INCLUDING MONEY & HOST OF THE DISRUPTIVE ENTREPRENEUR PODCAST

"Raw, Honest, Inspirational, Transformational. This is such a raw, honest book that you will want to keep listening and reading many times over. You'll find yourself nodding and ahh-ing with the occasional hell yes thrown in too. This book gives you permission and encourages you to look deep at your current beliefs, the ones holding you back and then gives the practical guidance and tools to change them so they work for you not against you. Anna is truly inspirational and this book is transformational and one that I highly recommend and will also be gifting many of my clients. "

TRACI CORNELIUS

"It deserves more than 5*. Thank you so much Anna for an incredible book that had honest and invaluable content that can change so many lives. You are so inspiring and authentically incredible role model to how a mentor and coach should be.

I am an NLP practitioner and during my training 4 years ago I struggled to use certain techniques but the way you used examples, it was so simple and I'm using this on my client exact same way.

In addition the strategies on using social media, no one has ever given so much value as you have, it's literally life changing for a business owner like me. Thank you so much. Highly recommend to buy!

NAZMA KAHTUN

"This book came into view just at the right time for me. Anna's story grabbed me from the start. The ambition, drive and frustration she shared were all too familiar. As a professional with a successful consulting firm, looking from the outside you wouldn't imagine I'd have any issues with visibility. I'm very confident and credible in my field, but branching sideways into a new niche and my inner critic reared its ugly head. Combine that with changes in my life, personally and health wise, I found myself self-doubting and shifting to a more introvert and reclusive version of myself. Yet as Anna talks about if you know you want to make a bigger impact with your work, you need to get visible.

With this book, Anna has tackled head on issues around identity, confidence, fear of failure and imposter syndrome, all quite typical in the online entrepreneurs niche, while also providing practical help with tools and techniques. She helps you to swap self-limiting beliefs for self-supporting words, to find your voice and get your message out to the world, online and offline.

With insightful empathy and a clear guiding hand, I totally recommend Get Visible to anyone whether introvert or extrovert. Now in pursuit of my visibility goals, I'm eagerly awaiting Anna's second book on podcasting, which once again is arriving at a point I'm planning to start a podcast series to support my business."

JAY ALLYSON, AUTHOR OF *LEVERAGED CONSULTING*.

"I didn't think I was a fan of Anna's work. I have followed her on Facebook and her podcast - there is some really useful stuff in there but I was quite triggered by the way she delivered her content.

But through this book and exploring why it was so triggering for me has in fact led to some huge breakthroughs - especially the audio book which I have listened to (I then went and purchased the book).

It has led me to question why all my school life I was creative and was going to go to art collage and I didn't. In fact I haven't done anything creative work wise since. That is going to change in 2020 as I explore what being creative means for me. I am pretty successful in my career and visible but I have learned so much and understand myself so much better through this book. I am quite blown away. I have a stack of personal development books on my shelf.

This book in many ways is a personal journey and that vulnerability is why it is so powerful and resonates.

I challenge you to read it."

M. ELLIS

"Thank you for getting visible..every word resonated with me and reignited something in me to step up to use the skills i have as a women's leadership coach and senior leader in a national charity to support the third sector that i love, have built my career in but can take its toll on the passionate women who work every day to make others lives that little more hopeful. Driven by your words 'anything is possible when you get visible' ..and as you say we don't do this alone. The balance of personal story, practical tips to help become visible and tools to work through to build own vision and confidence were great."

SARAH TITE

"Insightful and Inspiring. I can not recommend this book enough. Anna Parker-Naples takes you through her own journey, including the highs and lows, and how she's utilised these for her success. This is a perfect book to help you feel inspired, motivated, and ready to become visible, influential and ready to take on the world. Be ready to go through a range of emotions as you read each chapter and fall in love with the drive & motivation behind Anna's story."

JEMMA MALONE

"So inspirational. This is a really good easy to read book on making yourself visible as an entrepreneur. Lots of useful tips and tricks and the authors honesty about her own journey is really helpful to the reader. At the end of the book she helps you with pod casting and awards which is really insightful. Great for anyone launching a business"

VIOLET M.

"A great guide book to growing your business. So much practical advice in this book, plus Anna's inspiring personal story set alongside. I've used it as my guide, whilst launching a new business. Thoroughly recommended."

M. MCCOOK

"Brilliant. Anna always delivers. This was such an insightful read with. Lots of notes taken away to implement."

REBECCA COCKIN

"WOW, This is life changing!

I started reading this book thinking it would be about Anna's journey being in a wheelchair to success as an actor and coach.

What I really didn't expect, was to learn about NLP and so many 'drop the mic' moments with our everyday thoughts patterns and language and how we can truly change our future by noticing and being more mindful of this.

The book has end of chapter exercises for the reader to work through which is so powerful!

This book would be so powerful as a group book club read too!

I hope this is just the start of a series of books from Anna as she has so much to give to the world! Thank you Anna!! From a fan in Derbyshire!"

EM SHARPE.

"Finally a book that I get!

Sometimes I will buy a book hoping it will take me where I should go. This book took me to beyond this and more.

We so often take things for granted, not realising this is the easy stuff. This book shows you a bigger picture. It does what is says on the front. Great book, finally found a book that I can work to!"

AW

"What a fantastic book! It is full of Anna's story, her struggles and so much valuable content on how to beat your fears of visibility. There are lots of exercise in there to help you dig deeper into your thoughts and I have had some valuable insights which will change how I play out in my business going forward. Do not hesitate to buy this one - well worth the investment!

KINDLE CUSTOMER

"A must-buy for all entrepreneurs and business leaders. 5 stars!!!

This helped transform my business. I was already doing well but I wanted to increase my reach and connect with my existing customer better as well as reach new customers. The insights were incredible and I was able to clarify what my business was about and then start communicating more clearly with the right audience. A must buy for all entrepreneurs and business leaders. 5 stars!!!"

JOANNA MESSENGER

"A must read for any entrepreneur wanting to break through those fears and get visible. I absolutely loved the raw honesty of Anna's journey in this book. To be told she'd never walk again and now only a few years later to be inspiring so many is enviably sensational. This book was also incredibly practical. I'll be recommending this to many others."

CATHERINE MORGAN

DEDICATION

To my family,
who keep me grounded
as I reach for the stars.

PROLOGUE
THE DECISION TO BECOME VISIBLE

Hidden, limited and invisible. I sat in my wheelchair feeling overlooked and miserable at a New Year's Eve party. I was surrounded by friends celebrating their bright futures. The juxtaposition of their excitement and zest for life jarred with my dark personal situation. I knew as midnight struck that I had to do something, anything, to alleviate the depression threatening to consume me. I'd dreamed since I was five years old of being known, recognised, applauded for my talent and abilities but life had taken some unexpected twists and turns. Instead of standing in the spotlight, centre-stage, here I was, forced to sit, feeling frustrated, small and unseen.

I made the decision to change, and what I learned along the way was so utterly life-altering that I feel compelled to share it with you. I was not satisfied playing small, or, if I'm honest, not playing at all. The story of my journey to visibility encompasses major realisations about how I was holding myself back. I now understand through coaching hundreds of talented creatives, coaches and entrepreneurs on how to gain the recognition and success they desire that many of my fears and private shames are universal. The truth is that anyone can choose to be visible, seen and heard.

And I *did* choose. I chose recovery, forward-thinking and achievement. Becoming visible consciously and deliberately was the cornerstone to transforming my sense of fulfilment, my professional achievements, my income. Along the way, a dramatic turnaround in my thoughts allowed and enabled my physical recovery. I permitted myself to go full throttle towards opportunities with a sense of adventure - free from the fear of success, free from the fear of failure - and as a result I found myself on red carpets in Hollywood, I found myself on international stages as a headline speaker and I found myself a multi award-winning business coach and entrepreneur. All of my plaudits, all of my highs come down to this − *the decision that it was time to get out there and shine*. To really be me, no holds barred. To cultivate ways to be seen and no longer hide my light.

Visibility is about raising your kudos with deliberate and intentional strategies in order to effect more impact. For me, there are three major keys to visibility - *being seen, being heard, being remembered*. Whatever field you work in, you can increase your results by raising your visibility in your industry and in your local connections, much like I have done. What I'm about to show you in this book works for all sorts of people – entrepreneurs, performers, coaches, authors, artists, health and wellness businesses, fitness services, taxi companies, bloggers, consultants and IT professionals - anyone who is ready to stand out from the crowd to gain better results for their business. Success is measured in many ways - financial reward, freedom of lifestyle, personal fulfilment, loyal clients and a tribe of the right people around you, industry recognition … or maybe just doing what you are passionate about and sharing your worth with the world. Visibility gives you options. Instead of *chasing* connections and opportunities, you'll find they fall in your lap because you have done the groundwork in becoming known for your specialism. When you are clear and specific about who you are, what you do and for whom, it is easy for others to know when to come to you for help, when to recommend you, when to connect with you to book your services, when to ask you to be a featured expert. It is easy for you to increase your impact and sphere of influence.

If you wish to change your corner of the world, affect lives, increase your own income or brand yourself an expert, then you need to be visible. In order to run an effective business, become an author or speaker, or simply up-level the results you get and the amount of clients you reach, it's crucial to ensure you're known for what you do. Becoming the go-to person in your field is totally achievable when you understand and apply the right business processes and together with an awareness of your mindset.

Visibility has never been easier to attain than now, with the plethora of social media platforms available to us. Opportunities abound if you know how to seek them out. Yet many who want to lead a bigger life, who crave the adulation, success and recognition that visibility brings with it are also scared to raise their profile. Being seen presents the possibility of judgement from friends, family, strangers. From that girl you went to school with who was just plain nasty. From the old colleagues who treated you like dirt. From your sister-in-law sneering down her nose at you.

Getting out there and showing the world who you are and what you do requires courage and confidence. For many, some major hurdles need to be leaped. I know that, and I understand it because I've had those fears too. I'll talk you through exactly how those fears kept me stuck, frustrated and limited, and how overcoming them made me see opportunities and possibilities I had overlooked out of ignorance and self-sabotage. I'm going to show you in this book how to overcome your own fears around becoming visible and the limitations you've placed upon yourself without knowing it. I'm going to give you the foundations to implement a strategy to become valued and valid within your industry, whatever work you do.

If, like me, you are a book lover, then you'll know that

there are books that are more than mere books. There are books that shift us, transform us, awaken us. There are books and stories and words that lift and inspire, that shape us back into who we were always meant to be. I see so many people full of potential hiding in the shadows of their own ability. I watch talented, switched-on individuals shy away from the spotlight out of fear or out of a lack of knowledge about how to claim the stage for themselves. A part of them wonders why they haven't 'made it'. Yet. They don't realise they have an abundance of opportunities to carve their own mark on the world right in front of them, that the impact they yearn for is theirs for the taking. If only they would wake up and see it.

Since you are reading *this* book about getting visible, I'm going to assume it is because you feel you don't have enough of a profile yet, that you are dissatisfied with where you are at in your life right now … with the amount of recognition and reward you are reaping in your professional world. Your finances are suffering, you fall short of making useful connections, you pull back from marketing or putting yourself forward in some way. You're aware that you block yourself, but you don't really understand why. You don't know how to change … it's just the way you are. Maybe you blame others for your lack of progress - it's not your fault, you've tried but failed. There are reasons, there are excuses. But something nags at you - a feeling that you should be doing something more. I'm guessing that you feel a sense of greater potential lying dormant but which echoes through your heart, through your being, pulling you to *do* more, to *be* more, to impact the world in some way.

I felt that pull for a long time and personal development books helped me to begin the long process of self-recovery. I was recovering from myself and the limitations I had unwittingly placed on my abilities to achieve, to be seen, to be heard and to be remembered.

During my early twenties, whilst undergoing training as an actor at drama school in London and ready to begin my theatre career, I discovered my first self-help book, Julia Cameron's *The Artists Way*. It was my inaugural lesson in the ability to choose to think differently, to acknowledge and overcome past emotional hurts, to move confidently towards a bolder version of me, the version of me in my dreams. Or more correctly, the version of me that didn't pull back and limit myself in order to fit in and be accepted. The version of me that was more than ok with standing out from the crowd.

I had become scared of showing people who I was. I was dimming my light so as to *not* outshine those around me. I'd known since early school days that girls my age were often intimidated by my potential, and that felt painful and led to a fear of rejection. I pulled back and hid parts of myself. Finding Julia's book and discovering I was not alone in feeling that I had a capacity for greatness was one of those lightbulb moments I shall never forget. Marianne Williamson's quote also resonates with me: 'It is our light, not our darkness, that most frightens us. Your playing small does not serve the world. There is nothing enlightened about shrinking so that other people won't feel insecure around you.' I'd unconsciously played myself small.

Fast forward twenty years. I am now a multi-award-winning performer recognised for my skills in Hollywood and a multi-award-winning business and mindset coach. I am an international motivational speaker and host of *Entrepreneurs Get Visible Podcast* (no.1 in the iTunes charts alongside my heroes and heroines – Tony Robbins, Amy Porterfield, Gary Vee and Marie Forleo) sharing my message about living out your dreams and ambitions. Much of what I teach is about the practicalities of becoming well-known in your field. Knowing I wanted to spread my message wider, I attended an event hosted by Hay House Publishers, world leaders in personal development publications. The writers' workshop had a special guest - Julia Cameron, the author whose work had touched my life decades before. Now in her 70's, she asked the assembled workshop participants: 'What kind of book would you share with the world if you didn't have to be afraid?' I realised then that I wanted to share my story, warts and all, of going from feeling invisible, small and unhappy to becoming creatively and professionally fulfilled, recognised and validated, *visible and invincible*. So - whilst the content of this book will give you countless tips on how to get ahead for your business, it all starts with my own journey to choosing to be seen.

Not everyone understands the call to *do* more, *be* more, *have* more. Many people around us are prepared to settle for a comfortable, smaller life. And that's OK. What's important, though, is that you choose not to stay small to fit *their* model of who you should be. That you take action to protect yourself from people who do not support, understand or appreciate your dreams, and receive solace and shelter from those criticisms in those who *do* 'get' what you want and encourage your bold, courageous actions - be that in communities, podcasts, courses or books.

I want you to be honest with yourself about the size of your deepest hopes, goals and ambitions. I want you to face up to the personal hurts and professional frustrations you have encountered. It's too easy to pretend that your wildest imaginings don't matter, to dismiss them as pipe dreams. The truth is that you can't break through to another way of living and expand your life and business if you don't admit to yourself that you DO desire success, recognition, growth and impact. You have to admit to yourself that you want to be seen and heard, and that you are ready to smash through your fears about doing so.

What would happen if you did start on the path leading to a higher, more connected, more purposeful life? What would happen if you knew your value and worth, both financially and on a more impactful level? What would happen if you shared your worth with the world?

What would happen if you were SEEN? I'll tell you what. Your life and your business ventures would be limitless, and you would awaken those around you to their potential, too.

I hope that this book will inspire you to greater expansion in your world … that it will encourage you to step outside your comfort zone and go after the big ambitious dreams you harbour inside. I hope that this is one of those books you'll remember in twenty years' time, that my story and learnings will help you to step up and lead a bigger life, and give you the courage, confidence and know-how to get visible.

When we step up, we unconsciously give permission to those around us to do the same. This is a sentiment that echoes around my mind, as a paraphrase of Marianne Williamson's writings.

It's time to come out of the dark, step into the spotlight and get visible.

It's calling you. You hear it.
The whisper in your heart
The echo through your being
The pull from deep within your belly.
You are meant for more.
The place you have been hiding, seeking safety from pain,
That dark corner, in the cupboard under the stairs,
Cramped and tight, felt comfortable for a while, familiar.
It is not where you were born to live.
You are meant for more.
You lift your head and see the light spills through the cracks around
the doorframe.
You look closely and realise the door is ajar
It is open, waiting for you to be brave enough to walk through.
It always has been.
You were meant for more.
A strong, loud, silent voice nudges you.
Now is the time.
You have everything you need.
Come out of the dark.

1

INVISIBLE FEARS

On a balmy November night in Hollywood, standing on the red carpet as a celebrated awards finalist, I was hit by a realisation. I had a message and story that I needed to share with you, with other ambitious, entrepreneurial, creative, capable people who are fundamentally just like me; with people who want to have more impact, more success and more recognition but don't know how to make that happen.

Standing in front of the camera, under the dazzle of the photographer's spotlights, dressed more glamorously than ever and experiencing the most intense feelings of belonging and achievement, I saw how far I had come in just six short years. I had gone from disabled and depressed, feeling invisible and severely limited, to achieving industry recognition on a global scale, creative fulfilment and financial acceleration. I felt invincible with a rock solid mindset and an awareness of the power I had to expand my life. This transformation came as a result of the darkest of days and sheer desperation. Having reached out for help with my physical disability and depression, I made the most important discovery of my life: the power of *mindset, words* and *language*. I was set on a path I could never have imagined. I left pain and hurt behind as I sought and achieved the stellar creative and professional success I craved.

Struggle and frustration

Much like you, I used to struggle to find ways to be recognised for my talents and abilities, and to get the financial results that I wanted. I had no concept that the way I was thinking and behaving was behind my failure to achieve my dreams. I was talented, attractive, capable, ambitious. What was holding me back? I told myself, and anyone who would listen, that my lack of success was due to a lack of opportunity, money and professional and familial contacts. In short, it was everyone else's fault but mine. Now I understand it was something much closer to home that had kept me from fulfilling my ambitions. It was me, myself and my underlying lack of self-belief.

And now, here was I, a 'normal' (what does that even mean?) mother of three who spends most of her days juggling a busy household and doing the school run in Bedfordshire, Southern England, standing in Los Angeles, fully recovered and healthy, being celebrated for my talent in a highly competitive niche creative industry. Not only that, but wearing a cracking pair of high heels, strutting my stuff on the red carpets of Hollywood, USA - I mean, come on! Hollywood! And walking in heels! The stuff of impossibility just a few short years before. As the photographer snapped away, I awoke to my story's potential to inspire others to change their lives much like how my own had changed. In that instant, I made it my mission to share what I have experienced with others who feel stuck, limited and frustrated in their creative and professional lives … and teach them how to get visible.

Frustration and unhappiness aren't just about work, are they? Frustration bleeds into the rest of our lives, too, because our work and our ambitions feel like the heart of who we are. If you sense that your potential is unfulfilled, then I want you to have the knowledge I've uncovered. I want you to have the epic success that you deserve by putting into practice what I have learned. It doesn't matter what industry you're in, or if you want more money or validation from your peers, colleagues and your industry at large - you can make it happen. Just like I did. I've used everything I've learned about getting visible in the voice acting industry to replicate my attainments in other fields. I've used my experience to grow an international coaching business and to being celebrated as Business Woman of the Year & Entrepreneur of the Year at national and regional levels. I've translated my learnings to winning awards amongst celebrities for my ability to inspire people. Seriously, if you'd told me that within a year of launching my self-development business I'd win an award alongside singing sensation Adele and internationally-renowned football legend Rio Ferdinand, I'm not sure I would have believed it. Except that I *had* realised what was possible. I had chosen to stop playing small, and when you decide to be the strong, powerful person inside you, you can achieve anything you set your mind to. And so I duplicated these attitudes, behaviours and actions for my new aspiration, this time to become a motivational speaker. Within a short space of time I landed on some incredible stages, speaking alongside some powerful, well-known individuals, all from scratch with no contacts. I've proved that the techniques I'm about to share in this book work, no matter what field you are in. In my 1-2-1 coaching, in my group programmes and my membership, I've seen astonishing results in clients who have decided to face up to their limiting beliefs and become a well-known and respected authority in their field.

You see, I understood that choosing to achieve massive success starts with your own self-belief and is compounded by tiny steps of brave action over and over. I want to share with you where to start and how to continue changing the results you get. This matters to me - this is the impact I can have on the world. This is my ripple effect. My darkest, deeply personal lows and my brightest moments can act as a beacon of hope and possibility for you. If you ever see that photo of me on the red carpet in Hollywood, LA, you'll see that I am glowing with a new determination. It is that drive that has led me to write these words. And to you reading them. In these pages, I want to help you to understand how you can go from feeling invisible and overlooked to standing out from the crowd, recognised, connected, confident and VISIBLE.

Childhood decisions

Let me take you back to the very beginning.

There I was sitting upright in school assembly, arms folded and legs crossed on the polished parquet floor like a 'good' girl. I can recall the feeling of injustice when our headteacher announced that only specially selected members of the school, including children from my class, had been chosen to take part in a school production. They had been working on it secretly for many weeks and would be performing in a proper theatre for the whole of our county. I was indignant and hurt. Why was I not chosen? I was capable, I worked hard, I was just as special as those boys and girls on stage. It was more than an injustice. It felt as though I was SUPPOSED to be heard, to be seen, to show everyone what I was capable of doing. So why hadn't I been given a chance? Why had no-one recognised *my* potential?

As children we are encouraged to dream and to think big. We're told we can do and be anything we want. At what stage did you begin to believe you couldn't? For me, it was the tender age of five. I recognised a dream to speak up and be seen, but I felt aware of another need. To fit in.

From that assembly onwards, I would find every opportunity to read aloud, play the recorder in class, sing, dance. I KNEW I was meant to be in front of an audience, and that sense of knowing drove so many of my decisions. My guess is you've felt that too, being aware and understanding intuitively that you are meant to be doing more, leading a grander, more impactful life. Am I right? It's often hard to admit these desires to those around you.

From primary school I relished saying words out loud. I liked the attention my voice could command. It felt natural and easy, like I was in flow somehow. And yet when I looked around the class, I would witness my classmates' struggle with the exposure. They would become embarrassed, stumble and flush with awkwardness. They would keep their hands down when asked to volunteer to get up in front of the class. I would hear them say they didn't want to do something that would make them feel uncomfortable. I learned, too, that being the centre of attention, the show-off, the egotistical brat speaking up in class was considered by my peers to be a bad thing. In order to be who I wanted to be, to do what came naturally and what felt right, I had to face being different. My actions were driven therefore by two separate desires: to fulfil my potential … speak up and be seen - versus the need to be the same as everyone else. These two parts, unknown and unidentified, lurked in my unconscious mind and played havoc with my confidence for the better part of the next 30 years until I reached the lowest point of my life.

Whilst sitting in that wheelchair, heavily pregnant, disabled and depressed at a fancy dress party on New Year's Eve, the sense of desolation and despair was overwhelming. Resentfully I watched everyone around me celebrate the festivities - the women dressed in various Batgirl, Wonder Woman, Super Girl and other sexy outfits - full of laughter, excitement and fun. I sat feeling fat, frumpy and deeply ashamed of how I looked and felt. Of how small my life had become, and how small it would now stay. I had chosen for my husband and myself to turn up in the costumes of the characters Lou and Andy from the hit comedy show *Little Britain*, which meant wearing a shabby vest top and baggy, scruffy jogging bottoms. In truth, that outfit was all I had worn for a couple of weeks. I had stopped looking after myself as it hurt too much to get out of bed. I had long since given up washing my hair properly. It seemed pointless when all I was going to do was sit in bed all day, isolated and in pain. Getting to this party, where I stayed for less than half an hour, had been a gargantuan task. Encouraged by my husband and parents that it would do me good not to mope and dwell on my sorrows, I had shown up … but my heart wasn't in the party spirit. On my head was a wig that was bald on top with long, straggly ginger strands at the back and sides. I couldn't have looked more unattractive if I had tried. The joke in *Little Britain* is that every time Lou, Andy's carer, turned his back or left the room, Andy would jump out of his wheelchair, run around the room and dance. Ironically, this was in stark contrast to my dire, trapped situation.

One week earlier I had been given the news that I may never walk again. I had a pregnancy-related condition called SPD (Symphis Pubis Dysfunction) and it was the most extreme case my hospital consultants and midwives had ever encountered. It affected my pelvis, my back and my legs, and left me unable to bear weight without excruciating pain. For many mothers, SPD is a common complaint in the last few weeks before birth. For me, it was a debilitating, life-altering issue. Not only did this physical limitation mean that I was facing a life of pain, it meant that I would not be the kind of mother I wanted to be (mother of two young children with a third on the way), the kind of wife I wanted to be (newly-married just six months before), or live the kind of life I had expected, that I felt *entitled* to. I would not be returning to the stage, to the career I had put on pause to have my family. I was full of rage and frustration for the injustice of it. It was more than an injustice: I was *supposed* to be heard, to be seen, to show everyone what I was capable of doing, not sit here full of potential that would never be realised, living much less than half a life. I knew I had to find a way to make peace with the darker, limited future I was facing before I fell down a void of resentment and anger from which there might be no return. I decided that once the baby was born, I would seek help with how low, stuck and limited I felt.

That help was the catalyst for changing my entire life, and from those lowest of lows I lifted myself to the highest of highs. Recognition in Hollywood was beyond my imaginings and yet that's where I found myself. And since then, my aspirations, achievements and attitude to life have been even bigger and more adventurous. In this book I shall explore with you what I learned from encountering NLP (Neuro-Linguistic Programming) and embracing all things 'mindset' into my new world; how it altered everything, and how you can use what I have understood to transform your own life - personally, creatively and professionally. I will demonstrate how you can be more comfortable reaching out for success and recognition and how you can make the decision to DESERVE to have more influence in your chosen field.

Unfulfilled

I'll bet that you have reached out for this book because there's a part of you that is frustrated with your current reality. Perhaps you are not yet on the path to fulfilling your potential. Maybe you're working in the wrong field just to make ends meet. Or maybe you are on what once felt like the right road, but your *mojo* has gone and you're no longer making headway. If you're like many entrepreneurial and creative people I know, you have tried other avenues to satisfy your wants and needs but something always niggles at you. You are meant for more and you are tired of playing small. You are ready to grow. It is all well and good knowing that you want more, but how exactly do you play big when no one knows about you, and you haven't got the money, contacts or know-how to 'make it happen'? Well, those are all things I believe I can help with.

I'll explain more about how that feeling of being unfulfilled kept me stuck for many years in my early acting career, and what happened for me when I began to unravel my deepest fear - that I did not belong, that I was not 'the same' as everyone else. *Belonging* is a primitive need - to be accepted by the tribe and to be loved by those around you. For our cave-dwelling ancestors, these drives to belong and be accepted were essential for survival. In our modern world, we have the same drive and psychological need, but find ourselves quashing our biggest hopes and ambitions in order to find approval. Except we don't find approval within ourselves. We blame everything and everyone around us for us not having fulfilled our potential. What we don't acknowledge is that it's most often our own self-beliefs that keep us stuck.

I used to feel utterly resentful of not having the success, recognition and results I felt I deserved when I was a working actor (or more commonly a 'not-working' actor) in my early adult years. I had talent, I was more capable than many of the performers I encountered, so why was I not being booked for the jobs I wanted? It did not seem possible that I was meant to fail. After all, I could feel IN MY BONES that I should be on stage - so why was I constantly rejected? I had no inkling that my own actions, thoughts and behaviours were sabotaging my results.

When I was 26, I found myself unexpectedly pregnant. At the time I was working as an actor (or about to begin rehearsals the next day) living in London. When not touring with a theatre company I temped in the offices of the Square Mile, the area known as The City of London. I did some mind-numbing jobs to pay the bills, working in many different corporate fields such as Insurance, Underwriting, Shipping, Human Resources, Accounts, Training and Development. I was lucky to land a lot of auditions - some pretty high-profile ones – was always shortlisted, rarely selected. For several years I felt as if I was on the verge of a breakthrough. It was inconceivable that I would fail as an actress: I received fabulous feedback from directors, producers and fellow actors. I was as determined and ambitious as any young performer could be. I'd recently been working with a small touring company, performing in smaller roles in an ensemble production of *Macbeth* on the proviso that I would play the coveted lead role in *Romeo and Juliet* for the next tour. We'd be touring the UK and Ireland with ample opportunity to get casting directors to come and watch. In fact, I'd already done the leg work to persuade a couple of agents to come and see me on opening night. However, my value system was about to come into play in full force.

Seeing the blue lines on the pregnancy test, I knew my life had altered once and for all. No longer would I be gracing the stage as Juliet for the next 12 months (my producers really weren't keen on the idea of a Juliet some-what noticeably 'up the duff'…). Instead, I assigned myself to the new role of stay-at-home mother.

You see, I had these firm beliefs that it was impossible to be a good actress *and* a good mother. And that meant that the role of motherhood, higher up in my value system, won hands down. If I was going to be a mummy, I wanted to do it to the best of my ability. It didn't occur to me that I could do both. Right there and then, I closed the doors on my creative and professional aspirations. Or at least I did whilst the baby was small.

What happened, though, was that whilst outwardly embracing all things about being a mum - and the strongest part of me adored that new role in my life (after all, family was and still is my highest value)- the part of me that was full of potential and talent felt stifled and unhappy. I was stuck, limited and frustrated and I would talk about it all the time, constantly justifying why I didn't have the career I wanted, why I wasn't successful, why it was important to me to be at home with the baby. I felt judged in some way for having failed, except I didn't realise that *I* was the one judging *me*. I did not comprehend that the beliefs I held about performing and about being a mother were self-imposed. All I saw was that I could never have the success I craved *and* be the kind of parent I wanted to be.

I embraced all things about being a mother with small children, and those years flew by in the way they only can with little people to care for. And now, with a reception-aged school girl, a 13-month-old toddler and a third baby on the way, with pregnancy complications causing me to become disabled, you can fill in the blanks on how I coped after being told that I would never walk again.

In desperation I went to see a hypnotherapist. It wasn't the first time - several years before, stress had manifested itself through not only sleepwalking, but often getting up and putting on every single item of clothing I owned before getting back into bed. I would think I'd seen giant spiders whilst I slept. One night in a deep sleep I was convinced that one such spider had landed on my husband's cheek so I 'delicately' brushed it aside. Or so I thought. In actual fact I had punched Geoff hard in the face. It was decided that my sleepwalking and lucid dreaming had become intolerable and I sought out a local hypnotherapist to help me. It worked. After one session the spiders had gone and my stress abated (and no more punching my husband whilst he was out for the count, you'll be glad to hear).

Fast forward a few years and I was ready to learn

ANY ways to cope with my disability and open to anything that might improve my mental wellbeing. Hypnosis seemed an obvious choice, given how it had helped before. Truth be told, I was so down, so lost in the fog of my own misery and chronic pain that I would have tried anything.

Neuro-Linguistic Programming

The conversation with the practitioner that day changed everything. I did not know it then, but it was my first introduction to NLP (Neuro-Linguistic Programming) which shares many connections with hypnosis. Through a conversation around my frustrations and unhappiness, I managed to unlock parts of me that had been shut away for years. It was like a mirror being held up reflecting my thoughts, my words, my language and behaviours.

For the first time I was made aware of how much I talked about pain and being stuck. This seems an obvious thing to talk about when you are experiencing pain, but what I came to understand was that pain and limitation had become my dominating thoughts, and my predominate topic of conversation. When my husband came home from work, I would tell him I was in pain. When my parents helped with the children, I would tell them how sore I was. When a friend came to help me out, I would claim I 'was always in agony'. In the session I was encouraged to examine these words and statements. Was it true that I was always in pain? What about those moments when my attention was elsewhere, when I was happily watching *Jeremy Kyle* or *This Morning* or better yet, *Eastenders*? I tried those moments on for size. What had I been thinking about as I watched Jeremy Kyle? It wasn't pain - my attention was directed at the programme, pain wasn't in my awareness. It was like a truth bomb dropping. It was not true that I was *always* in pain. There were moments when pain was not in my awareness. Other things were happening to me. 'Always' was an exaggeration, an embellishment. It wasn't true that I only had pain and disability to think and talk about - I just wasn't giving the other things my attention. Lightbulbs were flashing in my mind and little did I know it, but new neural pathways were being formed…

And then came a more compelling question. What if the doctor who told me I may never walk again had been wrong? I had never questioned this. Doctors have power and influence – we trust their authority. But what if there was a possibility that I could recover, and quickly? Again, I had become so locked in my story of how much was over for me that I had never stopped to consider the possibilities of healing and recovery. I was asked if I knew of any instances where people with severe physical disabilities had gone on to walk again or gone on to achieve greatness in some other way. And yes - I did know of people who had transformed their lives through abject hardships. We all do. I was even being treated at Stoke Mandeville

25

Hospital, the original home of the Paralympics, where people with injuries far worse than mine were often to be seen practising for their super-human feats.

I was challenged - what would happen if I changed my language emphasis to healing instead of pain? What would happen if I focused on the things I *can* do and that I *do* want, without allowing self-doubt or fear to creep in? What would happen if I ceased talking about limitations and resentments and started looking for opportunities and growth? It dawned on me that I had believed for many years - certainly long before I had children, and perhaps even before I began my career as a performer - that I would not have success as an actress if I wanted a family. I would not earn decent money as a performer, and as a white middle-class British brunette I was not sufficiently unique to build a solid career. Behind each of these limitations hid the big fear − fulfilling my potential, being seen and heard, meant I would not belong. The bigger and brighter I grew in potential and success, the more I would be rejected by those I love and the wider society around me. On an unconscious level I had decided to continue failing. It was safer. It does not make sense to read it now on paper, but I can confirm after years working as a mindset coach and Master NLP Practitioner I now know that this is one of the biggest fears and limiting beliefs affecting people. It was the reason for the push and pull in my own career. It was why I would go all out to prove that I *deserved*, that I was good enough … whilst at the same time displaying a lack of conviction that showed itself in the way I interacted with others and through my body language. My unconscious mind was busy at work giving me the outcome I expected - that I would be rejected, overlooked and invisible.

Opening up to possibilities

This was **BIG STUFF!** That one **NLP** session opened me up to a world of possibilities. I, and I alone, was in the driver's seat of my life. If I could change those attitudes and self-beliefs, I could achieve anything I wanted and more. And it all began with words.

The more these unconscious beliefs unraveled, the more I could see that the sense of belonging and community I had always wanted was there for the taking. The professional recognition I desired for my talents was available to me. The opportunities to connect with my industry peers and leaders were right in front of me, as, in fact, they always had been. I just needed to focus on making it happen rather than dwell on all those factors out of my control.

At core, there were three big revelations.

1. I could create a sense of belonging for myself.
2. I could create a sense of being enough for myself without outside approval.
3. I could stop pushing and fretting over what

others might think of me, which meant I could have more fun and take more risks.

I could start believing that anything was possible even if I was a mum, and that it might even make me a better parent along the way. I could start believing I was in charge of making high-level connections. I could start believing I could earn well whilst still being at home. I could seek out evidence that it was all possible and find people who had achieved that balance. I could reprogramme my thoughts, attention and behaviours to get the results a part of me knew I was capable of.

When we are stuck in a cycle of negativity, it's easy to know what makes us unhappy. I knew being stuck made me unhappy, but I did not realise that complaining, resentment, frustration and blame not only affect mood and emotion but can have a longer-term impact on the unconscious mind. This part of the brain is always listening and will seek to bring to your attention more instances of what you focus on. So - if you complain (like I did) about being stuck and frustrated, then that is what you'll experience and pay attention to. If you say that you always land on your feet that too will be what you notice, and what you experience more often. I had become accustomed to saying I was stuck and frustrated and that I had failed. My unconscious was listening, and then that limitation became a physical experience as well as a mental and emotional one. When I deliberately changed my language from pain to healing, something astonishing happened. I started to focus on possibility and change. I thought all the time about how active I wanted to be and the kind of life I wanted to live. I stopped speaking words of limitation. I began to be aware of less pain. I told myself over and over that I could heal. In a few short weeks I was strong enough to leave my wheelchair, at first using a zimmer frame to keep steady and then to using crutches. This reversal of my physical limitation filled me with hope. Changing my language and words had already made a dramatic difference. I became the walking proof that mindset work works. Literally.

Every day I chose to see opportunities that might be available to me, where before I had blocked them or not noticed they existed. I took charge of the success I wanted to have, and without negative thought patterns I became creative, visible and more widely-recognised for my abilities.

Within weeks of getting back on my feet I discovered I could work as a performer from home if I focused on voiceover work. The voiceover industry was largely online so I could work remotely from my wheelchair (if I didn't recover fully) and participate in high-profile projects all over the world. I could be a leading performer working on commercials, audiobooks, radio dramas, video games and still be at home to do the school run. Oh, and I could earn good money doing it. By discovering that I could heal my body through my thoughts and words I saw that I could also transform my creative and professional success.

Finally, I acknowledged that I wanted to be successful, creative, ambitious, achieving AND at home with my children. I stopped pretending it didn't matter to me. It was only through changing those limiting beliefs about these two apparently conflicting concepts and adjusting my thoughts and language that I saw how I could use my potential. The same transformation is possible for you. That's what I want you to explore.

What do you want?

As I said before, we become so attuned to what we're not happy with in our lives. What would happen if you started to focus on what you *do* want? I know the answer. You can achieve the kind of things that currently you can hardly conceive of. I began by looking at what I was no longer willing to accept in my life. I created a new list of what I did now want to experience and altered my choice of words to enable new pathways of thought to develop and deepen. This is the process I want you to follow, too.

Without having a guiding point ahead of you, it is pretty much guaranteed you won't get there or indeed anywhere close. By creating a fully-rounded idea of where you want to head in the biggest, grandest sense for your business and your life, it becomes easier to break goals down into achievable targets and consistent actions.

I was accustomed to talking about what I could not have and how stuck I felt. Once I stopped saying those phrases and focused on what I *did* want and the ways in which I had the freedom to choose and explore possibilities, amazing things unfolded, and quickly. I decided that I wanted to heal my body and my mind, that I wanted to win awards for my talents, that I wanted to be at home with my children and that I wanted to have fun in my work. I wanted to allow myself to dream big and go after those goals without fear or constraint. I wanted to elevate my status, kudos and standing and become visible!

As living breathing humans we are bombarded with experiences that can make us unhappy, upset, sad, frustrated and angry. I shifted from thinking about bracing myself against searing hot pain and to thinking of a warm, nurturing, healing glow. When I had the urge to complain, I bit my tongue and said something positive or kept quiet. At home we implemented a new routine of speaking about my physical limitations. Instead of moaning and justifying my lack of ability to do simple tasks, and effectively going on repeat about how terrible my life was, I was permitted only to say to my husband once 'I'm having a healing day'. This would be his prompt to have conversations with my parents, my friends, my carers about what needed to happen to look after the children that day. Rather than filling my mind and speech with my sorry saga, there was now space in my head for other thoughts and possibilities and for more fulfilling conversations. My body responded by releasing much of the tension I held and I began to feel better within a few short days. My energy levels changed, my outlook on life altered and I saw choice and opportunity where previously I had only seen rejection and failure.

The trouble is, we have become so accustomed to telling a story of what we don't want that we often have little idea of what we *do* want. If we constantly talk about the bad things in our lives, the repetitive cycle of 'do not wants' gets stuck in a loop. Our mind quite literally throws back at us what we have been focusing on. So - if you're often saying out loud that you always mess things up, then your unconscious is going to help you find more ways in which to prove to yourself that you mess things up. The part of your brain that runs your internal systems is always looking to replicate the strongest messages it is sent. If the strongest and most prevalent thoughts you are giving out are detrimental to your life and wellbeing, that damage, limitation and sense of lack is exactly what you will experience.

Conversely, if you begin to tell a story over and over of how great your life is, how lucky you are and how easily and often things go right for you, that will, over time, become your experience. You might wonder how … and think that sounds a bit far-fetched. Well, the reality is that if you tell a positive story about yourself your brain then starts to sift through every encounter or interaction that you have had in order to seek out the best bits. And your mind starts to notice that there are many of them. Gradually your life experience improves simply because you are focusing on the fact that you are already open to noticing the happy, pleasant occurrences in your life. This change makes creating a future that fits what you want and building a business that you love - doing something which you are passionate about - much more of a possibility and not just some pipe dream. What you pay attention to becomes your experience, your reality. Focus on all the red items in a room, and you won't be aware of all the blue items. You've deleted, generalised and distorted what your senses bring to your awareness. You've filtered the world as you perceive it because of the instruction you have given your brain - to search for red. I had been programming myself to notice limitation for many years.

Negative patterns

We have all had a friend or relation who is convinced that they are unlucky, who thinks they are treated badly by everyone around them. We have noticed the amount of times they find themselves repeating the same mistakes in different scenarios. This is because of the recurring, powerful, negative thoughts they have about themselves. They are literally drawing into their own reality the confirmation and belief that they are unlucky, unloved and mistreated. And I'll bet you've noticed your own thoughts and words reflecting what they say when you're in their company. Maybe you have found yourself adjusting to their negative frequency with tales of your own woe, just in order to keep the conversation flowing. Perhaps you've come away from that encounter feeling worse than when it started! Get stuck on a negative frequency and it can be hard to shake off, especially if you do not appreciate the effect it has on your own world view. Equally, surround yourself with people who are happy and excited and it can be a challenge not to be lifted by them.

What does this mean for your future and how you can get visible? Well, if you can begin to tune in to the thoughts and feelings that will support your increased visibility and the things you want to achieve, you can begin to experience a new way of thinking about your future and what awaits you. You can begin to see opportunities when you decide that you are looking for them. For example, you will be open to hearing a message on the radio about a new event or you will find the exact quote that you need in a book. Your mind will be tuned in to all the new possibilities ahead of you instead of all the doors that you for so long considered closed.

For me, this manifested in how I discovered that voice acting work could tick all of my boxes. I stopped saying: *I can't* and began to say: *How can I?* I knew I no longer wanted to feel small. I no longer wanted to be limited. I wanted professional recognition. I chose to create thoughts that would enable me to take action on my goals and dreams.

Let's examine more closely what you have in your life right now that you do not want to have in your future. These can be massive clues for where you need to shift your thinking … and useful indicators for where to begin designing a future that fits with *your* wants and needs.

Activity: Reflections

Take a few moments to think about what makes you frustrated or unhappy with your life and work. Be honest.

I do not want:

I do not want these things in my life because they make me feel:

Activity: My future

Now focus on the kind of future you DO want to have. For the sake of this exercise, let any limited thinking just drift away. Allow your imagination to fly.

The way I want to feel about my future is:

Feeling like that about my future would mean the following for myself and my business:

I know I have been hiding by not doing the following:

I am scared to put myself out there more because:

Sometimes we are fearful of the things we really want to do. We worry about what others would think, whether our parents would approve, whether we would be any good at it and how we would be judged. These thoughts are often so ingrained that we do not even realise they are holding us back and yet they linger in our unconscious mind, playing havoc with the other part of us that comes alive when we are passionate about something.

Activity: Your Dreams

The following questions are designed to help you explore your fears about being, doing and having more than you experience in your present life. You might be surprised to see how much you have been holding yourself back from the activities you love doing and that make you happy:

When I was young I had this mad, crazy dream that one day I would be known for:

That dream was important to me because:

If I had made that happen, my life would be:

The reasons that this did not happen are:

The people who supported me and believed in me were:

They showed their support and encouragement by:

The thing that ruined my chance to do this was:

If I had a chance to do this now it would mean:

When I think about accessing that creative part of me again, I just can't believe that:

My deepest fear about opening up to that part of me is:

If I were able to fulfil my potential, I would be:

And if I had that in my life, it would mean:

If I were more visible it would mean I could:

Staying hidden means that I cannot:

Name your dream. That's right - if you were to fulfil your potential, how would you be spending your time? What would make you happy? WHO would you have to be? Which qualities would you be accessing from your natural abilities?

Dreams and success don't come to fruition on their own - you have to take action free from the fear that you do not deserve to attain them. In the next chapter we'll be diving into the limiting beliefs that you're dragging unwittingly around with you - much like I did for years - and I'll show you how to make sure you are totally confident, comfortable and fully aligned with going after the recognition and success you know you want. After all, if I can go from disabled and depressed to rocking the red carpets in LA, then anything is possible.

2

GET WHAT YOU BELIEVE YOU DESERVE

There is no point going after massive success if you don't believe you deserve it. There is no point pursuing a dream of having more impact if at core a part of you doesn't believe you will achieve it. This is the reason some ambitious entrepreneurs and creatives do not reach their goals. They are sabotaging their own results. For every progressive step forward taken confidently, crippling self-doubt and fear pulls them back. I should know, I've been there.

I'll bet you've experienced this too, in one form or other, though you just might not have recognised your behaviours or patterns. We often can't see in ourselves what is patently obvious to the outside world. Take one of my clients - I'll call her Rosemary. She's an extremely capable life coach and aspires to have both a thriving practice and an online, global impact. Her skills and abilities are innate and intuitive and her clients gain life-transforming results that allow them to feel happier, more content in their relationships and to have the confidence to charge more money for their own work. Her work quite literally changes entire lives in a few short sessions. In her own words, the transformation she provides people with is revelatory and worth potentially hundreds of thousands of pounds in increased earning over a lifetime.

Yet Rosemary feels deeply uncomfortable about charging a proper fee for her life-changing sessions. When she first came to work with me she would charge her clients a minimal fee and then feel awkward about the money exchange, so would on occasions not ask for the money at the end of the session. Or would hurriedly give a discount there and then in case the client hadn't yet noticed substantial improvement in how they were feeling. These actions were led by fear … fear that she wasn't good enough, that someone would 'catch her out', that if her ex-husband discovered she was earning good money he would find a way to shame her. She played small and couldn't understand why her business wasn't thriving and why it was so hard to increase her income. Her behaviours and actions around charging came from a desire to continue hiding to avoid shame and ridicule from those who know her. Her deep-rooted belief that she was terrible with money ensured she gave her powerful services away for next to nothing.

Another client of mine works in television presenting and has done for the best part of 20 years. She is well-known in her field, well-liked and respected. She is, to the outside world, highly successful. However, in her own mind, Vicky is full of self-doubt and carries an ongoing dislike of any of her peers who she perceives as getting booked to present instead of her. This resentment carried over into the connections she made in her industry. Once we established the limiting beliefs Vicky held about her own fears and how this sense of competition had become toxic for her mind, thoughts and feelings, we were able to work out how to eliminate or counteract those thoughts and behaviours. In fact, the level of resentment Vicky experienced often gave her migraines and caused her to cancel bookings at short notice, which in turn affected her reputation for reliability. Watching Vicky realise the effect of her own actions was like a light being switched on. It hadn't been her 'competitors' that were preventing her from getting more bookings, it was her own actions. We worked to overcome this and Vicky began to see how much she had held herself back. No more. Tired of feeling second best, Vicky realised that she had been scared to win presenting jobs in case others resented her. Now she understood that she could be a role model and mentor for others joining the industry rather than focus on her own sense of rejection.

Take another extremely talented, creative lady … we'll

call her Val. She is capable, intelligent, great with people but lacks the confidence to charge properly for her work. Others get ahead of her and she is almost always broke. She could earn thousands if she chose to but instead is stuck in a cycle, feeling resentful for the peanuts she makes. It is frustrating to watch.

Vicky, Rosemary and Val are not one-off cases and my own story echoes the fears I witnessed in them.

I want to share with you my deepest fear and how it held me back for so long. I will admit that there is some residual part of me that still has these fears and when I'm hormonal for one week of the month, these are the darker thoughts that seep through into my actions and behaviours. Thankfully, with all of my mindset knowledge and experience, I am able to recognise them, take stock, adjust those thoughts and forge ahead. For many years I did not have that awareness.

My limiting beliefs

Remember that NLP session that I went to? Well, it set me on a whole new path of going after what I wanted. It changed my life so much that I created an incredible career, from home, being around for the children, working on high-profile projects all across the world as a talented, recognised performer. Many of my boxes were ticked.

Wanting to learn everything I could about unraveling these thoughts, I booked a six-day course to train as a

NLP practitioner. On the first day we were asked to choose a belief we no longer wished to have and were prepared to let go of. One participant chose the thought 'I can never lose weight, no matter how hard I try'. Another chose to let go of, 'I need a cigarette after I've eaten'. With much greater awareness of some of the thoughts wiggling around my head, and by now years of journaling in a stream of consciousness manner thanks to Julia Cameron's book *The Artist's Way* (more on this later) I knew that a thought that plagued me was that I did not belong. I would go to parties and social events with friends and feel like I was on the edge of the group, that no one really 'got me'. I would go to auditions and feel over-looked and unnoticed. At school I never quite felt a part of things even if outwardly I appeared one of the crowd. I wondered if it stemmed from being the only girl out of four siblings. I was different, I didn't fit in. I've since come to understand that this is one of the most common limiting beliefs that people hold on to unconsciously. I spent a lot of time ruminating on why I didn't fit in, why people didn't like me, why I felt excluded. In my mind it was about how *other* people treated *me*. I had focused on interactions where I felt rejected. I would arrive at parties and observe all the conversations that I wasn't a part of, or that I didn't feel welcome to join in with. I'd always considered myself confident but I would hold back, away from the thick of the action. I was always on guard for moments of rejection. Don't get me wrong - it didn't stop me from letting my hair down. I thrived on one-on-one conversations, *deep and meaningfuls*, rather than surface level chit-chat. I would still have a good time but part of my brain was working to point out to me all the people who hadn't spoken to me, or where the rapport hadn't flowed - further proof that I was an outsider, that I wasn't liked, that I didn't fit in. I was deleting all of the evidence that I was part the crowd, accepted and welcome.

So for this exercise I identified the thought that I did not belong. I considered 'I don't fit in' to be a fact, simply who I was. After all, there was an entire back catalogue of circumstances where I'd been ignored, sidelined or rejected. It had been my chief focus. The ramifications for my life were huge. Professionally, creatively and in my personal friendships and relationships I sought rejection and braced myself to receive it. I bolstered myself against these hurts before they even happened, a kind of mental armour in preparation for attacks.

I'll be honest. As I began the exercise I did not believe that I could get rid of the belief that I didn't belong. It felt like the fabric of my being. It dawned on me, too, that I had been encouraged at home to believe that I was a bit different and that that was a good thing to be relished, to be proud of. Except I didn't feel proud. I felt excluded and resentful. I couldn't fathom how a simple exercise could change this. However, NLP techniques had helped me recover from not being able to walk. I had also believed that I could not have the success I wanted as a performer and at the same time be a devoted stay-at-home mother, and I had smashed that belief out of the park. In fact, the day before the course started it had been announced that I was a finalist for two awards in Hollywood. The industry recognition for my talent that I had craved for so long had finally come. I'd posted on social media that I was excited by the impending awards, which in part I was. It's not every day you get to tell the world that you're going to Hollywood.

However, when the trainer asked us to introduce ourselves and what we do, I was crippled with embarrassment. The trainer questioned why I was playing myself small. She'd seen on social media that I was a finalist in Hollywood … why wasn't I talking about that, owning my success? I flushed, deeply uncomfortable. Why, now that I had the recognition I'd craved, was I embarrassed in a room of strangers?

Two things were going on: 1. I didn't want to be so very different from the others in the room. I wanted to belong. In fact, I had already decided that I did not, that these were not 'my people', that there would be no common ground. 2. I was a bit scared of going to Holly-wood. On the one hand I knew that I was good enough, that I stood out, that my work was of a high standard, that I had worked my socks off to get there and had a library of work to back up my achievement. But what if someone realised I didn't really belong there amongst the best in the industry? What if I was found out? What if I wasn't good enough? What if I was exposed as a fraud for all my hustle, hard work and confident exterior?

Clearly I needed to work on my sense of belonging and deserving.

The potential to belong

We were asked to close our eyes and bring to mind an image of what we did not wish to have as a belief about ourselves any longer, to really notice what popped into our heads - sensations in our body, any little thing that became apparent to our minds. For me, it was not just an image. It was a pounding in my chest, a sound, a smell, words and association. What came up for me was a strong, fully-formed image of an event in my teenage years. I saw it in full technicolor glory. The colours, the details, the freckles on the faces in front of me. There was fear in my stomach, panic and adrenaline coursing through my body.

What did my mind most associate with not belonging? A specific event when I was 16 years old. I was attacked by a gang of girls from the other side of town, a moment that affected me deeply some twenty years before. It was powerful, compelling evidence that I did not belong, that it was necessary for me to always be on guard for rejection, hurt, humiliation and shame at any given moment. As a result, I lost my confidence, many friends and acquaintances. It also led to some rash decisions about my education in a bid to leave my hometown as quickly as possible. In many ways it was the moment I grew up and left innocence and childhood behind.

Here's a description of the image: I'm standing in the high street, in the town that I've lived in since I was two years old. I know no other hometown, this is where I belong. Out of the corner of my eye I can see the school I had attended years before, a charming building at the end of the High Street. It was a happy place for me on the whole. I felt a part of things and my dreams and ambitions to perform were supported there. In fact, as I write this, I've been invited back as a motivational speaker for the middle-school leavers awards evening, revisiting the stage I found my voice on aged nine when I first had a taste of speaking in front of an audience.

Directly in front of me and filling my frame of vision is a girl, a year younger than me. I know her by reputation but have not met her before. I know she is violent. She is as solid and bulky as has been rumoured, a giant beside my tiny body. I can see her freckles, the flecks and blood vessels in her eyes. I can smell her breath, the cigarette she's recently smoked. I can see the intention on her face to do me harm, as she leers in and says she's been sent to teach me a lesson … that no-one likes people with big mouths speaking up and sharing their opinions. I can see many other teenage girls around me, perhaps fifteen, perhaps twenty, closing in, surrounding me, and I can hear them chanting my name, laughing, ready for the 'fight'. I've never seen any of them before, but I know who they are. Everyone does. They're part of a family and extended connections that most youngsters in our town know to avoid. They are trouble, and I am surrounded. I can see two of my friends who have run to a distance, scared for themselves, keeping themselves protected. Most of all I can feel the panic in my belly, the surge of adrenaline tingling right through me to the tips of my fingers, the pounding in my chest, the roar of blood in my ears as everything in my life has led to this moment of terror.

To give context to this Saturday afternoon on February 16th, 1994, I need to take you back to two days before. I'd arranged to go to my good friend's house and as we were as attached to our parents' landline phones back then as my daughters are to their mobiles today, I called her first. I discovered that her new boyfriend would be there when I arrived. *New* by just five days. This boy, like his family, was notorious in our town. He was one of the youngest members of the family and already at 15 bad news. Most of us wanted to stay at arms' length. I told my friend that I was concerned for her. I'd known her since I was five and we had been close for years. She was one of my best friends. In fact, our mothers were close friends too.

Most of our circle had decided to keep away and wait for this latest romance to fizzle out. However, since I was due to go to her house, and he was there, I told her how much we feared being around him and asked that she be careful not to get mixed up in anything dangerous. I spoke up, I used my voice, I expressed my fears and I looked out for a friend.

The problem began after the call. She told him what I had said and I was later informed that he had taken it upon himself to ensure I learned my lesson. Since he considered himself gentlemanly, he would not 'kick the shit out of me' himself, but rather offer his many female cousins and their sidekicks the pleasure of attacking me. My friend colluded by informing this gang of my name and crucially where I would be on Saturday (meeting her and other friends in town). She even phoned my two companions 30 minutes before the attack to ensure I was definitely going to be at our usual meeting point at the specified time. I walked into a trap laid especially for me. Whilst I prepared for my standard Saturday afternoon trip to the High Street, ready to hang out with my friends, perhaps treat myself to a new top in Tammy Girl or a new Rimmel lipstick from Boots, these individuals were sharpening the edges of their sovereign rings with metal files.

The image that sprang to my mind for this exercise was the split second before the first attack to my face.

The rest is a blur even now. My next vivid memory is after I had run away – how, I do not know - to our local Shell petrol station. The attendant locked the door and called the police, the ambulance and my parents whilst I hid in the toilet. I had to see my face, to see the damage that had been done.

It was a shock. Beneath the blood streaming down my face a piece of my lip and inside of my mouth was totally gone, ripped out, probably sliced off by one of the sovereign rings. My face was disfigured. I felt sick, devastated, distraught. As I looked in the mirror there was all the proof I needed. I was rejected, I was not safe, I did not belong. I was not loved, I did not fit in, I was not respected. I should not speak up. I should keep quiet … and I should be cautious of my friends.

I thank my lucky stars that a talented doctor, skilled in facial reconstruction, was on duty in A & E that day. Those wounds eventually healed and within 10 years I was hard pushed to see the external damage, although even now the scar tissue inside my mouth reminds me of that attack.

Some 20 years later I had pretty much forgotten that experience. And yet I now understand that it had been filed away at an unconscious level as a constant red flag that I did not belong and had to keep myself safe. It affected the level to which I trusted other friends, and the level to which I trusted in relationships. It drove my decision to get as far away from my hometown as possible, despite my loving, supportive family being there. It drove my decision not to reapply to the Royal Academy of Dramatic Arts, when, after a series of auditions for drama school and reaching the final rounds at numerous prestigious and highly-regarded actor training establishments, I received rejection letters. The rejections felt like a smack in the face (notice my language here: it's a bit of a give-away to what these feelings were associated with). I was rejected, I did not belong, I did not fit in, I should keep quiet and hide until the trauma, shame and humiliation passes.

On the surface I was a confident, go-getting, ambitious young woman but there was a distinct fear bubbling away inside that showed up in discreet ways. It kept me closed to taking risks and stepping outside my comfort zone. In workshop-style auditions at the start of my acting career I would push to be seen, to be heard ... but on some level this was out of a desperation to be wanted, accepted and noticed, to PROVE my worth. What's the best way to drive people away from wanting to work with you or be friends with you? Desperation, neediness and showing off. Despite having numerous *nearly-made-it* instances of breaking through with my acting career, I felt marginalised and overlooked. I would receive feedback at nearly every audition I went to that I was talented - so what was wrong? Why was I not landing the roles? Why was I not making the right connections with the right people? During the next part of this NLP exercise, I was to find out.

We were invited to envisage a belief we would prefer to have instead of this old limiting belief. My feelings and beliefs around not belonging were so strong, the only option was the complete opposite. For me, the new belief was that I was loved deeply wherever I was … that I belonged … that I was surrounded and enveloped by love and support. This time, when I closed my eyes, alert for any offering from my mind as to an interpretation of this thought *I belong*, what came up was a symbol of a warm, loving heart … fuzzy, reddy-orange … and a feeling of being embraced deeply. Physically, the sensations were comforting and uplifting, like a giant hug that goes on and on. The thoughts associated with it were of love, acceptance, joy and happiness. Focusing on this belief of *I belong* was compelling. It felt good - not just in my mind, but in my body.

The filing cabinet of memory

These images and sensations connect with how our minds store experiences and interpretations of events around us. Imagine your unconscious mind is like a set of four old filing cabinets. I tend to imagine them as vintage, probably from the 1940's. I don't know why I think of them that way, and I don't need to know. It's what my mind offers me and the analogy works. The filing cabinets are old, a bit dishevelled. A drawer is off its runners, a handle is missing. They are dirty, dusty and overflowing. Despite in principle being a filing system, there is no order, only chaos. It's a bit overwhelming to know that someone, sometime is going to have to face clearing the system up.

Where to start? Each file containing a memory is just stuffed randomly, often with information decades out of date that should have been shredded a long time ago. Papers are filed in random places with no obvious connection. Some folders are stuffed full and bursting at the seams and are so faded by the light that the typeset on the paper is almost unreadable.

Now imagine someone taking the time to unravel that decrepit filing cabinet system, fix the handle, shred the unnecessary out-of-date information and compile a helpful index system - colour-coded, modern and swish so that any users of that filing cabinet system can ascertain quickly what can be filed where.

To me, that's what mindset and limiting belief work is all about: refiling the system.

The habitual programmes of your mind

Over the course of each day we have approximately 60000 thoughts. To prevent our mind from overwhelm and expending unnecessary energy, we've cleverly created habits so that we don't have to consciously think through every single activity of the day. If we did we'd be exhausted. Responses become automatic, such as brushing our teeth, putting on our socks, driving our cars. Likewise, how we approach situations and relationships becomes habitual. We don't know why we behave a certain way, in fact we aren't aware of it, but over time we've developed habits and thought patterns that are like programmes running in the background.

In every second of our day, every day of our lives, approximately 2,000,000 pieces of information are available to our unconscious mind. We cannot possibly process everything that is brought to our five senses - there's only so much room in our filing cabinet and it is already overflowing. At a conscious level, we are aware of only seven pieces of information per second - perhaps the colour of someone's hair, the way it made you feel in your belly when they shouted, the smell of perfume. Maybe the taste of bile at the back of your throat, the sound of a car horn in the distance. At an unconscious level we can store up to 134 pieces of information per each second of an event. So … during trance you can recall other sensations in your body, the specific texture of your clothes, the feel of the cool air against your skin, a flag blowing in the background, a rumble of a train, a distant voice calling to someone … on and on until your sight, sound, touch, taste and smells have been catalogued into 134 segments. Remember, though, that there are two million pieces of information available. That means that there are 1,999,866 other pieces of information available to the brain to process that cannot be filed away. They have to be generalised, deleted and distorted in order to fit into an already overburdened filing system.

This is why, when 30 people take the stand in a witness box after viewing the same event, each might give a different version of it. Even colours and descriptions can vary greatly. Nobody is lying. They are each telling their own truth. Each has a different *frame of reference*, a different filing cabinet full of associations and memories that the event they witnessed has been filed into. Each witness has filtered, deleted, generalised and distorted almost two million pieces of information per second. There is no right or wrong, truth or untruth …each literally sees and experiences the world in a different way, through their own distortions and filters.

Through a simple process, my limiting belief of 'I do not belong' was then re-catalogued in my mind as a historical event, something that had happened in the past, that could never be repeated. The image that came to me for this was my wedding day - a strong image of a happy day, full of brightness, colour, laughter and background chatter. Clearly, it was a specific moment in history that could never be repeated exactly as it was.

This exercise helped me to understand how I file away my experiences. I could look at that picture of my wedding and see that it was bright, a moving image … as though looking through a photo album with the images framed as I turned the pages. And the images appeared distanced from me. In my body this felt breathy, my cheeks aching from grinning. I could hear 1940's swing music and the sound of chatter and laughter.

The image of being surrounded when I was attacked, however, was dim, a still picture, and I was a part of it, seeing the situation through my own eyes, feeling a ball of heaviness in the pit of my stomach.

I needed to change how I stored these images and connections. In my mind, I stepped out of the picture where I was attacked and viewed it as though looking through a photo album. I could move the sensation in my stomach up through my body and change the sensation to breathiness and a smile in my cheeks. I could release the heaviness. I could change the background sounds of the chanting of my name into the sound of chatter and laughter. It was a shift that took less than a couple of minutes. But for my life it had big ramifications.

I had moved 'I do not belong' to the part of my mind that stored information in the past. It was now catalogued as part of my history, no longer present. I cannot describe adequately the sensations this caused in me. But the exercise did not stop there.

We were encouraged us to bring to mind an image that represents what we *do* want to have. My image was the new idea that 'I always belong', with the heart that I described previously. We took note of all the significant ways that this new idea was represented in our minds - location, size of the image, colour, sound, sensations in our bodies – in my case, pretty much all of the 134 pieces of information that my brain associates with 'I always belong'.

Finally, we took the idea of something that is universal truth, that is always and lastingly something we believe. I used an image for 'we walk on this Earth', creating a picture of walking on sand, hot sand beneath my toes as the rush of the sea resounded in my ears and the warm sun made my skin prickle.

I was able to shift this new belief 'I always belong' into the area where I file universal truths. It has to be experienced to be understood properly, but let me tell you this: it has had a lasting impact on my life. The whole exercise had taken less than 15 minutes from first accessing the image of being attacked. Those memories were re-filed so that they were no longer part of a constant belief but stored as a historical event. My new belief - 'I always belong' - was catalogued with my other universal truths as something constant and always true.

My eyes were closed for most of the exercise, and as this is *deep* work, it involves going in and out of trance. Trance isn't quite what everyone fears from Saturday night television. It is something we do throughout the day, comfortably moving into daydream. This is when we process information in our minds without our conscious brain intervening. You know that Inner Critic voice that tells you what you're doing is ridiculous? Well, in trance, that part of your mind is dormant, allowing the messages to reach the unconscious. During trance, our unconscious mind is fully in charge, always on alert to keep us safe and protected - its highest directive. Although I see people pretending to be chickens or whatever else during a hypnotist's stage show, nobody would do that unless their unconscious mind wanted them to have that experience. Similarly, during trance, we would never give out information we don't want to give away. We're safe and in control.

Trance is comfortable …so when I opened my eyes it took a while to pull myself together. I was quite literally seeing the world in a whole new way. For the first time I saw how I had kept myself distant from others, how I had focused on an old belief that *I did not belong*. How I had deleted, distorted and generalised interactions to fit a programme that had been running unconsciously - that *I did not belong*. With that programme now re-filed, I could see opportunities to create communities, further friendships, reach out to industry professionals without waiting for rejection. In short, in that 15 minutes, I discovered that many of the painful moments in my past came down to a fear that I would be rejected if I spoke up, was seen, was totally myself.

Immediately, I felt more comfortable about going to Hollywood. There were now opportunities to create friendships, build trust and loyalty and experience connection. I could let my hair down and go with the flow, safe in the knowledge that I was accepted wherever I went, that I belonged … if I chose to.

The choice to belong

The effect on my career and personal relationships was astonishing. If I belonged, I could focus on all the ways people reached out to me, all the ways it was OK for me to get ahead, be seen, be noticed. Carving a successful career became easy. Longer term, it has meant that I have increased confidence in what I want to achieve and ultimately led to creating my first self-development business and becoming a speaker and podcast host. I was free to speak my own words, not hide behind someone else's. Whereas before I had been uncomfortable on camera, afraid that my face would be seen and I would be judged, now I no longer thought that way. Facebook Lives and off-the-cuff live videos have become something I relish. I always belong. I can choose what to do with criticism, because it does not floor me anymore. I accept myself.

I've since seen this process change many lives and be the start of a bigger transformation. There were other exercises that shifted deep limiting beliefs during my NLP practitioner training and even more so at Masters' level, but that first exercise dramatically altered my self-perception.

Protecting the Inner Child

It helped me to unravel other decisions I had made about myself. I learned that limiting beliefs are often shaped in our formative years, between the ages of six months and seven years, or in cases of trauma, such as my attack. Every time we have a similar experience, or one that is vaguely the same, we file it in the same part of our mind, each subsequent event compounding the effect of the rest, making us believe that this decision we have made is a fabric of who we are. It is not. It is a decision, made at an unconscious level to protect us. It served us well as a mechanism for some time, which is why our minds filed it in that way. However, over time, it has kept us stuck and is no longer the most effective programme for other parts of our lives to function well. The problem is, we don't know it is there until we do some digging.

The decision to limit ourselves often happens in our early years. We explore who we are, and we explore our creativity. We're excited and so we share our work and a bit of our ambition with someone we perceive to have authority. We *show* ourselves. Occasionally their response is spiteful, dismissive or hurtful. We decide this rejection means more than it does and we create a new limiting belief and a programme that becomes an unconscious pattern in our mind. In the same way that I realised I'd had a fear that *I did not belong*, I later uncovered that I had fears about my talents and abilities.

I recall teachers who criticised me, fellow students who had been unkind. I can remember the girl at school who mocked me. Each of these scenarios were painful and I took them to mean I was not good enough. It was not true.

I want to share with you an exercise to find some of your own painful moments and where your limiting beliefs might have come from. This work is crucial to creating a new sense of self-belief and deservedness.

When we take time to be creative (through drawing, painting, playing music, singing, even speaking up in class) and feel as though our work hasn't been received well, we feel vulnerable and exposed. We've shown a part of our real selves and were rejected.

Creativity is an act of sharing yourself with the world and in an education system that celebrates perfection and being top of the class, together with parents who may have placed more emphasis on getting good grades in more formal areas, we may feel as though our efforts at expressing ourselves are simply not good enough. At a young age we may decide that it is not worth the trouble, and that doing something creative 'just for fun' is a waste of time. We place less value on our innate skills.

Likewise, a student with a strong personality and natural leadership tendencies can be warned to stop showing off or be encouraged to be less 'attention-seeking' which, in turn, creates a limiting decision to dumb down or not be seen. Uncovering these wounds and hurts can be liberating. Psychologists have proved that we make many of our decisions about who we are and what we are capable of by the time we are seven years old. Do you believe now that you knew everything you could be by the time you were seven? Perhaps it's time to let go of some of those decisions. First, we have to unravel them.

This exercise seeks to uncover some old, forgotten

monsters that are lurking in your unconscious and fuelling limiting beliefs.

Creative monsters

Your creative self-worth and belief in your abilities is important. If you don't believe you deserve the success and recognition you desire, there could remain a feeling of not being enough, a feeling of being fraudulent - often referred to as *Imposter Syndrome*. When we undertook creative activity as young children, we did so without fear of failure or criticism. We were open, free and honest. We created for our own pleasure. There was no vulnerability - we just created, free to be who we were and free to see the world in our own way. Along the way towards adulthood, someone was unkind about our abilities, told us we were not good enough, and we chose to turn away from our artistic inner child.

As adults, we now know that such a decision was limiting. However, since we rarely step back and examine our thoughts and beliefs, we keep ourselves stuck in old thought patterns. For every event we have ever experienced we have retained certain information to do with the images around us, the words we heard, the feelings in our body … and we store them away. Opening that memory box can be freeing.

In my memory box, among many others, was 'Helen', a ten-year-old girl who told me I was embarrassing on stage, that the teachers only chose me because I was teacher's pet. She told me I looked like a goat and had the ugliest eyes she'd ever seen. Also in the box was 'Adrian', aged 11, a trumpet player who mocked my voice from the orchestra pit, telling me I sounded like a six-year-old and should just shut up and keep quiet. And there was 'David', who told me publicly that I would never be successful as an actor because I was too intelligent, that I would not be taken seriously. Each moment compounded the next in the filing cabinet of my mind, preventing me from believing I was good enough to go for what I really wanted, to speak up on stage and be seen, to have impact and visibility. To be known as talented. They made the natural skills something to be embarrassed by. Helen, Adrian & David were my creative monsters, informing the voice of my *Inner Critic*. Recognising their influence enabled me to choose differently. You, too, can choose to believe that you *deserve*, that you can stand up, speak up and be seen. In turn, this makes it easier to take action towards your ambitions. There's no need for fear, embarrassment or awkwardness.

Let's look at your memory box of personal injuries, hurts and slights.

Activity: Your creative monsters

Make a list of three people from your past who were critical of your abilities. These are your historic creative monsters and whilst the event has long gone, the memory and associations have not. They may very well be people you love and who are close to you. That's ok, just explore what injuries you suffered on the receiving end of their criticisms or slights:

1.

2.

3.

Look at each one of these individuals in turn and recall as much detail as you can about the event when the criticism occurred. Take each person on the list one at a time. Close your eyes and think about that moment. What were you wearing? Where were you? What did they say? Was it a look or a feeling you got? How did your body feel? Were there any significant thoughts in your head at that moment? Detail below anything you notice about the scenario:

Historic Monster Profile

Name:

What they were wearing:

Where we were:

When this happened:

What I showed them:

How I felt about my work before I showed them:

Their reaction:

What was said:

How I interpreted it:

How I felt:

The decision I made there and then about my capabilities:

How that has affected my creative and professional life:

What I now believe is true about my abilities:

What Helen, Adrian and David said about me, I kept as truth for a long time. Letting go of that programming changed everything, as I hope recognising the sway of your own creative monsters will do for you. It showed me that I had limited myself out of a fear of being *not enough*. We're **always** enough. It starts with believing it. That fear kept me small. I was meant for more. And so are you.

UNCOVERING YOUR THOUGHT HABITS

By this point in the book I hope you'll be more aware of the ideas, thoughts and feelings that cross your mind throughout the day and appreciate how much of your reality and sense of identity are influenced by them. Noticing the thoughts you have on a regular basis leaves you in a position of strength. You can decide whether they work for you, whether they leave you feeling good about yourself or whether you have been sabotaging your self-esteem at every given opportunity. This is crucial as you begin to go after your business venture by becoming more visible.

I mentioned earlier that the first personal development book I came across was *The Artist's Way* by Julia Cameron. One of the exercises in that book has stuck with me and I've adapted it in order to uncover the words and phrases I use regularly. I journal stream of consciously every morning, letting any and every thought that crosses my mind land on the page. This gives me insights into the statements I make about myself and my abilities. Spot the limiting statements you make about yourself and you're halfway towards rectifying the power they have over your unconscious. Noticing your habits can prepare you for positive changes in your life and empower you to *use your mind* to benefit your wellbeing. The benefits for your credibility and validity as you get more visible in your industry will stand you in good stead. I'll show you that how you think about yourself is entirely up to you … and I'll give you more positive choices for how you view the world around you.

A whopping 95% of your daily 60,000 thoughts are considered by top neuroscience researchers to be repetitive thoughts. In simple terms, you are having the same thoughts over and over again. The reason the brain allows us to fall into these habits is that they make it easier to function, leaving brain power and energy available for more important decisions that may be required later on.

Take, for example, making a sandwich. There so many types of bread to choose from, so many fillings, toppings - but the staple favourite of cheese and pickle wins time and again (or whatever it is that takes your fancy).

Or think about how you have a shower. You do not have to even consider how to give yourself a good scrub or wash your hair - you just switch off mentally and get on with the habitual process.

What blows me away, though, is that a staggering 80% of our repetitive thoughts are believed to be negative. These are often ingrained into us from childhood and as we repeat these negative thoughts, day in and day out for years, we don't even notice that they are there. At any point, we can interrupt those habitual patterns. And that's exactly what I'm going to encourage you to do. *Notice the patterns*, so that you can *choose how to think*. No longer will you be at the mercy of outdated patterns of thinking. You will be in charge of your mind so that as you build your business, a growth mindset and a deep-rooted 'I can do this!' attitude is at the heart of all your actions.

Journaling with intent

Over the next week, I'm going to ask you to create a new routine for yourself. If that sends you reeling into thoughts of:'I don't have time for anything else!' or 'how on Earth will that fit in with my routine?!' then I suggest that those thoughts are habitual in themselves and that you are accustomed to believing you don't have any time. How does that thought serve you? It probably doesn't, so why not give this a go anyway and find out what you can learn about yourself?

Activity: Writing a journal

The new routine involves writing in a journal every day for three pages at a time without stopping. Before we go any further, write down your initial thoughts to the concept of writing a journal:

The last time I wrote in a journal or a diary was:

I found this process to be:

When I was younger, I found writing a diary to be:

People who write in journals or diaries are:

From answering these questions you've probably noticed a host of beliefs you hold about journal writing. Those thoughts are themselves habitual, formed a long time ago. How about we change any negative thought habits for this exercise and try thinking a new thought instead? Like this one:

Writing daily in a journal helps me in all areas of my life.

Try it. You have nothing to lose (except some limiting beliefs!)

Your task for the next week is to find a slot of

time in which to dedicate to writing every day. Invest in a notebook with a design you love, or if you're feeling thrifty, use any paper you have lying around and just get on with it. The important part is in the actual scribing, the physical activity of putting pen or pencil to paper.

I suggest you write the good old-fashioned way. Don't type for this exercise. It is easier to become distracted once you open up a laptop or PC and there is artistry and mind-brain connection in putting ink on the page - a kind of freedom, a creativity in scrawling.

This daily writing will be a way to begin to observe your thoughts. You're not aiming for poetry or even a blow-by blow account of everything you have done that day, or that you plan to do. Instead, you are going for a *stream of consciousness* process. This writing is not for anyone's reading pleasure, so it does not have to have any artistic measure. It is top secret. It is not a record of who you are and where you have been and it is not intended as a biographical account to be handed down for generations.

It *is* a chance for you to record your moment-by-moment thoughts as they happen. Literally anything and everything that comes into your mind is worthy of being recorded the instant you think of it. For example:

I have a headache. I'm sick of headaches - they suck- it's always me isn't it? Life is so unfair. I think I've got some cereal left, but what about milk? I'm so rubbish I forgot to get some last night ... Oh my head ... Poor me.

What you are aiming for is total abandonment, honesty and freedom in what you write. This is your uncensored self that you are allowing onto the page. At this stage you are not even going to be reading the pages back to yourself, all you are going to do is **KEEP WRITING ON THE PAGE** until you have completed three whole pages. Even filling the page with: *I don't want to write today, I don't want to write today* is OK. 'Three pages? Why so many?' I hear you ask. Well, you'll find when you do the writing pages as part of a daily practice that something interesting begins to unfold.

After about a page and a half, some more significant thoughts begin to appear. The serious issues affecting your unconscious mind come out to play once the daily gripes and groans are on the page and acknowledged and once the habitual thought patterns have been uncovered.

The simple process of writing, no matter what your thoughts are, ensures that you do not run away and hide from what matters to you and that you are allowed to express your thoughts, feelings and ideas without fear of repercussions or recriminations - that you make your real self *visible*.

Remember, these words are for you alone, and you know you will keep them safe and away from prying eyes. In fact, you aren't even going to re-read your musings AT ALL for seven days. If you find that the words do not flow on the page, try these topics:

How I feel about running a successful business

My frustrations with money

Why I am scared of being judged as I get more visible

Why I'm afraid of failing

The reason I hold myself back is

Activity: Ask yourself these questions:

What do I fear about writing daily without censuring myself?

What do I think about writing for three pages without stopping?

What other resistance do I have to doing this exercise?

There are several benefits to this daily writing exercise:

It sets us up for the day, especially if we are able to write early in the morning. We can get our complaints and *poor me* thinking out without having to share them. We've had the thought, given it space and can then leave it behind.

After a few days we begin to see how many of our thoughts are repeated. Once we notice them, they have less power over us. Later on in this book we'll visit these repetitions in more detail and work out how to tackle them head-on.

The very act of finding time and quiet space to do the daily writing is an act of compassion and kindness towards ourselves. It is a way of acknowledging that our own needs, feelings and personal space are important … amidst our other duties and responsibilities.

Daily writing allows the creative, artistic side of us a place to rear its head in a safe and private environment. It may be that you want to use the blank page to express some of the beauty you see in the world around you, or to discuss how the music you heard on the radio made you feel. These all help to create new neural pathways in your brain.

Freeflow writing can offer a release from issues that have become blocked. It can give you insight into changes you have long wished to make and the impetus to finally take action in making your life happier. There are only so many times you can write the same frustration over and over without deciding that you need to take action to do something about it.

What do you need to do in order to make this daily writing happen this week?

What is the best time of day for you to write?

Where is the ideal place for you to write?

Sometimes, even when we know something is good for us and will set us on the path to establishing a successful business or to achieving a creative accomplishment, it is a challenge to actually take the actions we want to take. Making a firm commitment can make a tremendous difference to our mental fortitude. Below, I have compiled a formal commitment for you to fill in before forging ahead with this daily writing (by the way, if you do miss a day, don't waste time, effort and energy berating yourself for it, just make time to start again at the earliest opportunity).

My commitment to myself

This week, I shall make time and space every day to write my daily pages. I shall write for three full pages without censoring myself and allow whatever thoughts spring into my mind to be written on the page. I will be open with myself. I am committed to daily writing because I am ready to make some changes in my life. I acknowledge that by doing this daily exercise I am allowing myself to grow.

Signed:

Date:

This exercise can unlock hopes, dreams and ambitions … and more crucially the limiting self-beliefs that have kept you stuck. Once you hear the stories you tell yourself, you can acknowledge that they are not true and craft the more beneficial belief that you can do what you want, that you DESERVE to live your best version of you. You can have impact. You have it within *you* to take action and build the life, business and dreams you desire. Not only is it totally possible to become visible, but it is exciting and appealing to do so, safe in the knowledge that this is how you can reach those bigger goals.

4

DESERVING SUCCESS VS. THE INNER CRITIC

I, alone, am responsible for building my reputation. One thing I have learned in each field I have worked in (acting, voiceover, corporate, franchise owning, health & wellness, personal development, business coaching and speaking), is that if I want recognition, awards, recommendations, connections and referrals, it is down to me to ensure I am sufficiently credible to warrant them. The same goes for you. If you want people to shout from the rooftops about how good your services or talents are, *you* have to be *the one* to start spreading the word.

This is where many talented individuals fall down. They feel uneasy about talking about their worth, as though there is some shame in running their business or going after a career path. I hear it all the time - people saying they want to grow their business but stumbling when they have to tell someone about what they do.

Through my work in countless coaching sessions I now know the fears most often underlying the bumbling responses when asked, 'What do you do?' and the playing down of achievements and successes, or worse - not even mentioning the project and ambitions that mean the most.

If you do not tell people, clearly and confidently, what you do, you cannot build trust, loyalty and a positive reputation. Wherever you go, whatever your line of work or creativity, you are your personal brand. How you show up, how you interact and engage is what people remember and recall. If your fears are not dealt with, they will sabotage the plans and ambitions you dream of.

Take the fear of judgement. It prevents otherwise confident individuals from talking about what they do. Criticism and ridicule are avoided in order to protect the fragile ego. Marketing emails are not sent. In-person introductions are not made. Social media posts including successful achievements and testimonials are not shared. There are usually two parts to this fear. One is the fear that people at large will not like them, that they'll receive some criticism from an unknown community who will spot them for the fraud they are. The second is often a much bigger hurdle to jump - the fear of friends, family and old acquaintances knowing what they do and judging them as not good enough.

The irony is that most people do not care what you are doing. They are too wrapped up in the minutiae of their own lives to be interested. Yet it is the fear of condemnation from those close to you, who know you perhaps in a different capacity, that keeps you stuck.

Years ago, I read a blogpost on the amount of people who attend funerals. I forget where I read it, so allow me to paraphrase. At the end of your days, after spending many hours procrastinating over taking actions towards what you really want to achieve in life, concerned that you'll be judged not only by those who know you, but also by the multitudes that do not, on the day of your funeral, it is extremely likely that those people you have been so mindful of are unlikely to attend, and particularly less so if it is raining. If you live a long, healthy life the number of people potentially willing to don a raincoat and come and stand at your grave as you are lowered into the ground is just two. That's it. I love this story. It gave me a wake-up call. All that worrying about what people think … what's the point? If they don't care enough to turn up to give me a final send-off in death, why should they influence my life? Food for thought.

So - where do these sabotaging, undermining thoughts come from? This was a bit of a revelation to me, and I hope it will resonate with you on some level.

The prime directive of your unconscious mind

Your unconscious mind has your best wishes and interests as its prime directive. At all times, in all moments, it is on the look-out for your highest good. That's the reason you'll wake from a deep sleep if there's a potential intruder in the garden, the reason you'll arrive safely at a destination even when your thoughts are miles away whilst you drive. Your mind is always paying attention to what you feed it with. If you focus on dismal thoughts, it will search out more dismal thoughts for you to pay attention to. This is the same phenomenon as when you buy a new car, for example. You may think you've gone for an unusual colour and suddenly, as if by magic, you see the same make, model and colour everywhere. It isn't that there are more of them on the road … you're just paying attention differently - *distorting, deleting and generalising* to suit what you're telling your unconscious.

Taking you back to my recovery story - I stopped focusing on struggle and difficulty and began focusing – single-mindedly - on healing. I thought long and hard, and in detail, about warming glows and how good my body is at mending itself. My external and internal experiences hadn't changed, but my mental focus had. In turn, I noticed that I was perpetually focusing my thoughts on the career I believed I couldn't have, and with new awareness I sought instead to pay attention to all of the opportunities I had not previously been open to or aware of. If the nagging doubts of my highly vocal *Inner Critic* reared their heads, I would change my language and thoughts. I would visualise, over and over, the belief that would support my goals and ambitions.

As someone who has always been ambitious I was

curious as to where the negative comments inside my head had come from. I started that process of journaling and focused on the negativity that came forth as I wrote, and in so doing identified exactly what these limiting beliefs were, and any strong associations I had with them - images, memories, feelings and fears. One such image was of a theatre school director I had encountered aged 20. I saw him in my mind sitting cross-legged in his office, his tiny white dog on his knee resting against his belly. His half-amused tone and the way his long eyebrow hairs moved up and down seemed to feature in the way I was talking to myself. It struck me that whilst this man had always proclaimed that he had my best intentions at heart and believed in my talent and abilities, his actions and words often belied those statements, leaving me confused and bewildered ... doubting myself.

With further digging I uncovered a painful belief about my ability to write. I cannot tell you how long I believed the following to be true, and it is only through deep mindset work and understanding the impact an event that happened in my childhood had on my creativity and self-belief, that these words are down on the page now and that you are reading them. On a Brownie Girl Guide camp one summer, probably age seven, I was delighted to have the opportunity to work on the camp daily newspaper. I was going to be in print! At this stage in my life I wrote all the time - little stories, pretend magazines. I'd been given my first journalistic assignment: to produce an article on the Rifle Shooting activity. That evening the article was already in print and I was so proud of my achievement. I hadn't shown anyone yet and had big plans to send a copy home to my parents. Here was I, a published writer! I sat that evening typing my next article, ready to go to print in the morning, when the youth who had been running the Rifle Shooting entered the newsroom and picked up the day's copy. He read out loud my article and proclaimed whoever wrote it to be totally useless at writing. How dare 'they' say that his safety instructions were long and boring! He went on to pull apart - line by line - the article and author for lack of writing skill. I sat at the typewriter, adrenaline, blood pumping around my body, cheeks flushed, rigid until he had left the newsroom. I returned to my tent without the copy I'd planned to send home and gave up writing for pleasure for a very long time.

The limiting beliefs I carried around with me – the shame and embarrassment - I now know to be common amongst people who come to me for coaching. My deepest fears? *I'm not good enough. I'm not talented enough. I don't belong.* Any of those resonate with you? I'll bet they do.

Self-protection mechanisms

We develop these beliefs to protect ourselves from further hurt and shame. Our unconscious is doing what it sets out to do, keep us protected so that we can function and survive, and the techniques we employ have served us well for a time. They serve us until we realise that these limitations prevent us from achieving our higher desires, wants and needs. That fear of ridicule, judgement and shame keeps us stuck, doing jobs we don't enjoy and in relationships we know aren't right for us. But the decisions we made about our abilities at the moment of hurt, pain or trauma were not the truth. In that moment, we deleted and distorted so much information. I could, in that newsroom, have stood up and told him he was unkind and that his lesson HAD been as dull as I described. I could have made the decision to prove him wrong and to become a successful journalist or author. Yet I didn't. With the resources and experiences available to me, I had seen only one option - to absorb his remarks as fact about my abilities and to hide my shame by abandoning all hopes of writing.

After all, why would I pursue an interest if I wasn't any good at it? No matter what positive feedback I would then receive at school or at home, it was too late. This fear of being a fraud, underqualified or not as talented as everybody else kept me stuck, and I now know it as *Imposter Syndrome*, preventing people from going after their ambitions and creative dreams, fueling procrastination. This fear impacts marketing, networking, the ability to do a good job or even taking first steps towards getting started on the path of your dreams. Loyalty, trust and vulnerability are key components in building a following and being accepted as someone valid and valued within an industry, and if you are not able to spread your message confidently and clearly, you will sabotage your own success. Why does this happen? I put it down to the *Inner Critic*, that little voice inside your head. Whilst I might recall my theatre schoolteacher or Adrian the trumpet player, it isn't really *them* saying the mean, esteem-damaging remarks. It is *me*, myself and I.

Your Inner Critic is the part of your mind that tells you all the ways you're not good enough to go after what you want. Learning to take note of the comments and repetitive limitations that your Inner Critic sends your way can be career-changing. By being aware of these comments, and when they are likely to occur, you can diminish their intensity and the power behind the Inner Critic's intentions to sabotage your dreams, hopes and wishes. This is crucial as you up-level your business, when past conditioning can make it easy for self-sabotage to occur.

Once you recognise the power of the Inner Critic and the negative thoughts that do not serve in any way to improve your life and mental and emotional wellbeing, then you can choose to have better, more empowering thoughts, leaving you free to be more confident, capable and to achieve the success you want. Oh, and a lot happier and less stressed, too.

Have you ever noticed that just when you want to feel

your most confident, a little voice in your head is ready to remind you that you're not capable? Have you seen other people go on to achieve things you desire for yourself, but can't see yourself doing? Do you get caught up in visions of dreams not working out for you? Do you run visual scenarios of disaster? You are not alone. Most of us have some kind of internal dialogue between the part of us that wants to achieve, create and be free and the part of us that is scared, fearful and wants us to stay small, safe and protected (even if our current life is not satisfying or making us happy).

This part of you is the first to warn you that you are not capable, that you are foolish, that you are stupid, that your plans for your business are ridiculous.

We have become so used to the sound of the Inner Critic that we don't always notice it is there. Today, you're going to acknowledge your Inner Critic and the things it tries to tell you. In doing so, you can make new choices about what you listen to and how much influence that voice has over your life.

Our unconscious minds store all sorts of experiences and concepts - pictures, images, sounds, feelings - both as emotions and as actual physical sensations in the body, associations and metaphors. You will probably have a strong image or sensation from your Inner Critic, even if you have never considered it before.

Activity: Say hello to your Inner Critic

Close your eyes. Take a moment to think about the critical voice inside your head. Notice who it sounds like. Is it anyone you know? Does it appear on one side of your body (in your mind's eye)? What is it doing? What does it look like? Is it dressed in a particular way? Is there anything you can observe about its posture? Are any features exaggerated? Is it human, animal, cartoon or other?

Really focus on the information you have stored internally about this critical, negative part of you.

Jot down answers to the following:

My Inner Critic looks like:

It reminds me of:

I notice that it is doing the following:

Close your eyes again - this time notice if the Inner Critic has a voice that reminds you of someone or a tone that feels familiar. What kind of language does your Inner Critic use?

Notice if it starts to tell you that this exercise is ridiculous or a waste of time. Your Inner Critic is not keen on change or moving in a positive direction! Keep going regardless.

My Inner Critic sounds like:

Its tone is:

Its favourite sayings are:

Now repeat the exercise, focusing this time on the feelings within your body that the Inner Critic, and your associations with listening to it, create in you:

Where in your body is your Inner Critic located?

What is the shape and intensity of that feeling?

As you focus on your Inner Critic, take a moment to ask it what its purpose is. What is its highest intention for you? What is it trying to do? Why?

My Inner Critic's purpose is:

What it wants for me is:

What I have learned from this exercise is:

Acknowledging the voice and purpose of your Inner Critic can lead to the powerful realisation that often it is seeking to protect or help you in some way. Now that you recognise its purpose and aims, is it helpful to you in anyway? Perhaps its voice can now be quieter and you don't have to feel you are battling with it internally. What would it be like to be thankful for the role it has played in your life so far? Wouldn't it be great to reassure it that it has done a good job so far, but that you no longer need that protection?

Understanding where this voice comes from, and what it is trying to achieve, can go a long way towards unravelling how much it influences your actions and decisions from now on.

Activity: Turn those self-criticisms around

---

*Take the journal writing that you've done since the last chapter. With a highlighter, mark up every single comment or inference that you are lacking in some way. For example: **I'm so stupid … I always mess up … I'm rubbish at … Why do I always….?***

Some days you may have none of this self-criticism, other days your writing will be full of it. Just highlight every instance. You may be surprised at how many there are and the regularity with which they appear.

On the next page of your journal, write out each of those negative statements. If you have duplicates there is no need to write them out more than once (once is enough!) Just identify what your Inner Critic has been reminding you of over and over again. It won't be a pleasant read, however, you have the ability to choose which thoughts you give attention to and this is your opportunity to change how you feel about yourself. For every sentence on your list, write out the opposite of it. These are your positive self-beliefs.

For example:

I'm stupid *becomes* **I am capable and I am intelligent**

I'm rubbish at remembering to do everything *becomes* **I have a fantastic memory and I am doing a great job.**

I always mess up *becomes* **I often do things right and I am open to learning and growing when things do not go the way I hoped.**

Negative comments my Inner Critic wants me to believe and that have revealed themselves to me in my writing and my thoughts:

The positive self-belief statements I choose to focus on instead:

I expand on this exercise by writing each of the positive statements five times. As I write each line I'm often struck by that Inner Critic voice again, blurting out that I'm foolish, that it's rubbish that I can achieve, that it is all a joke. I jot that statement down at the bottom of the page and then go back to writing the five lines. In this way, I turn each of these 'blurts' on their head, always finishing with a positive statement. These become not only mantras that I repeat, but statements of intent for who I am becoming. I've spent too much of my life 'doing myself down'. I use these sentences to craft the self-belief that feeds my subconscious and creates new neural pathways in my brain.

Keep this list and add to it whenever a new positive thought about yourself occurs to you. This set of statements can become your intentions for who you are and a quick, easy way to build your confidence and self-esteem. Look at this list often and make it a part of your daily routine to give you maximum advantage in changing your business. To create the success you want, you have to listen to the part of you that knows you deserve it and minimise the impact of your Inner Critic as you take steps to become more visible.

5

CRAFTING YOUR CREDIBILITY

Nobody is going to award you with credibility, expertise and validity in your field without you doing some leg work. No one is going to give you permission to be bigger, have more influence or the potential for more income. The people you see as experts and leaders, the people you admire and follow in your industry have created their own credibility. They have deliberately and intentionally crafted their visibility. They have, consciously or unconsciously, given themselves permission to be seen and heard.

You can do the same. The process begins with deciding that you are headed for the top … that you will have a successful business and be a person of influence and connection.

According to the Oxford English Dictionary, credibility is: *The quality of being trusted and believed in.* For you, your personal brand and business, carving out credibility is about telling the story of why you deserve to do what you do, teaching and sharing what you know and the many ways in which you are valid (even if you are at the start of your journey there will be reasons for choosing that field and a lifetime of past experiences to back up your capability and commitment to your cause.)

Credibility matters because trust, loyalty and recognition within a field are the primary reasons someone will choose to initially follow you and later to work with you or buy from you, whatever your service or product. If you want more sales, more bookings, more recommendations and more connections, establishing credibility and making this a key part of your ongoing marketing efforts is paramount. People buy from people - more importantly they buy from people they feel that they like, know and trust.

As individuals, we shy away from revealing our vulnerabilities and imperfections. Paradoxically it is these human qualities that make us appealing, down-to-earth and trusted. As *Imposter Syndrome* thoughts and limiting beliefs make their presence known, we worry that we aren't good enough or sufficiently experienced to tell others what we do and why we are good at it.

To be known as the go-to person you do not need to know everything in your industry. You only need one or two levels of knowledge and experience above the people who look up to you. Sharing the learnings, struggles and challenges you have encountered are some of the most compelling ways for drawing an audience to you. You are not out-of-reach, you are a real human who is confident enough in what you do to share how you've overcome obstacles. Credibility is something that you can build and craft for yourself. It is about telling the story of your personal struggles, challenges, values, education and experiences (ranging from qualifications, credentials, life skills and technical expertise) together with your connections and relevant media exposure - to lift your presence online and chiefly to raise your standing in other people's minds. Every piece of content you create and post should be with the aim of establishing your credibility.

Marketing experts believed for a long time that we need to have contact with a brand or individual a minimum of seven times before they enter our awareness (NOT before purchasing - that comes later). In these days of social media that number is now thought to be close to 22-32 touch points before someone is aware of you and what you do. So - whilst you might think everyone knows what you do after posting a couple of social media posts, in reality, it hasn't sunk in or even been noticed! This is why shouting about what you do in online spaces becomes so important. If you do not tell people what you do, you lose out on valuable opportunities for future referrals and recommendations. Credibility is not just about the online space, though (although of course you can reach more people more often that way and for free). It is about what you say and how you behave when you network and meet people socially.

Crafting your story for effect

Storytelling is powerful. From now, I want you to start telling the story of why you do what you do and what makes you valid, capable and well-positioned to be able to do just that. If this makes you squirm, go back to the *limiting beliefs* and *Inner Critic* work in this book.

It's easy to recall and share our stories about all the things that have kept us stuck and why life isn't as we want it. Now is the time to carve a new life story. Every event in your past has brought you to where you are today: the good, the bad and the ugly have been part of your personal and professional growth and development.

You know you want more success, impact, influence and income. The way to do it is through careful, considered, authentic positioning.

This next exercise is one that requires some thought.

Activity: Your story

Write out all the parts of your life story that are connected with your business or the big, bold ambition that you hold dear. You might include decisions you made in childhood, past work experience, relationships. Or not. It'll no doubt be something personal that has shaped your path. Look at the significant events that have led up to now. Write it all out in detail, at least a couple of pages long. This work is valuable so take the time to do it fully.

When you stop listening to the limiting beliefs that you uncovered in the *Inner Critic* and journaling work, and listen more closely to the part of you that knows you are meant for more, it becomes easier to stamp out your expertise in a given field, even at the start of a new venture. You do not have to know everything and everyone in an industry to be valid. You have only to know where to find the next pieces of information.

The most appealing people we see on social media are often the ones who share their struggles, challenges and new learnings. If you are at the start of a new venture, how can you turn that to your advantage? How can you weave the story of why you are doing what you are doing? If you've been in your business a while now, how can you tell the story of your business growth and development? Can you share what you wish you had known?

Every experience you have been through has brought you to this moment. You might be an expert or the go-to person without even knowing it. Challenges or achievements you've had at school, work, in your personal life or business are experiences you can now translate into a positive learning for your future clients and industry peers.

Activity: My achievements

Below, I want you to list all of your achievements. Next to each one, write how this can be transferred to your new/current business or ambition.

Achievement:

How I can transfer this to my business:

In the next chapter we'll be looking in detail at who your ideal client may be. However, I'd like you to give some thought now to whom you might appeal as a role model. Is there a demographic for whom you could represent a powerful stand? Consider what you have achieved, experienced and learned and how it might relate to someone else's struggle. What have you overcome and now have a greater understanding and knowledge of as a result of that hardship?

Looking at yourself objectively - your hardships, your successes, your challenges, your wins - what kinds of individuals might you be a role model for? Who might be intrigued, moved or inspired by your story?

Whatever industry you are in, it is important from the outset to work out not only how you are the same as everyone else, but all the ways in which you differ.

Activity: What do I have in my experience toolkit?

Answer these questions:

What qualifications, associations or affiliations do you have within your industry?

What courses have you taken?

With whom have you studied or trained?

What has compelled you/motivated you to step up or change direction?

What was the lightbulb moment?

Who are you connected to in your industry?

Who have you met?

Who do you follow that inspires you?

What makes you different to other people in your industry?

What is unique about what you bring to your work?

Are there any well-known brands or companies that you have been associated with?

What makes you unique?

How can you tell that story?

Why should someone choose to work with you, connect with you, follow YOU rather than someone else in your field?

What do you know that others want to learn?

(Brainstorm and journal around this point, and add to this list - you will always be learning and growing and pinpointing the next thing you can talk about and teach others is important in terms of positioning).

Sharing your value, knowledge, passion and expertise and providing valuable content and information for the industry you are part of can be a fabulous way to build credibility. We're going to investigate the areas that you can easily talk about, teach and share ... the parts of your knowledge and passion that you are able to share with others. Passion is engaging and compelling and draws others to you.

Activity: Powerful content

Write down the top three things clients/friends/others ask you about:

    1.

    2.

    3.

What do you LOVE talking about and explaining to people about most? What lights you up?

How can this feed into your business?

If, right now, you had to talk about one topic for five minutes without stopping to think about it, what would it be?

Throughout the rest of this chapter, I'll be encouraging you to get more visible online, in-person and in the media. That can be super-scary - I know that. However, to get your business to a point where you can have the impact, income and influence you dream of, there are some mental challenges to cross.

The fear factor comes from those deep-seated limiting beliefs we have begun to uncover and dispel in the *Deserving* work we did earlier. In this section, we're going to explore them a little more closely and acknowledge they are there. When we cast light on them, these beliefs and fears have less power.

Activity: My fears

My biggest fear about getting more visible is:

The reason I am fearful is:

The person/people I am most scared of judging me are:

Our visibility fears are often closely linked with our ability to speak up and share our truths. In fact, public speaking of any kind is believed to be the biggest fear most people have, beyond even dying! Speaking your truth and being seen in the world as a mover, a shaker, a person of importance and relevance is something totally within your capability. Speaking up about yourself, your work, your ambitions, your successes is all part of engaging content marketing. Every post you write, every blog you create, every word you say on a Facebook Live, video or podcast, is going to be about you speaking your truth and being you - the *real* you - not some polished, pretend version of you.

The fear is your obstacle: *you* are your greatest hurdle.

What is your fear about speaking up?

Why are you afraid to tell your truth?

What situation in your past indicated that it was not safe to do so?

There will have been times in your life where speaking up and being seen has been safe, comfortable and rewarding.

Activity: When I felt good

Make a list of those times below:

How I felt when I was recognised for what I achieved:

This felt good because I knew that I:

Activity: Why my work matters

Now that we've acknowledged the obstacles, let's investigate why it matters to you to increase your influence, income and impact:

I know that I have untapped potential because:

The reason I am no longer prepared to settle for less is:

When I have more income I will be able to effect a change in the world by:

Connecting with people who respect and admire my work, both as peers and as potential clients, means:

Tips for creating an online presence

The first place to get more visible and speak up about your work and your capabilities is on social media. Being strategic, deliberate and consistent in your posts makes all the difference to your credibility in your follower's eyes. You will attract the attention of your peers, those who look up to you and those that you look up to.

As I write this, I realise that I hope this book is useful for years to come, and that in helping you to gain credibility, I need to talk about social media as it exists right now. If some of this has changed, I hope it is easy to translate the main points into whatever the social media landscape is by the time you read this!

I recommend that you target just one or two social media platforms in the early stages. Once you have them nailed (or you are in a position to outsource some of your social media) then you can move on to others. The main thing is that your profile names and profile pictures remain consistent, either as your name (rather than the brand name of your business) and if you prefer, or if your name has already been taken, the type of work you do. All of your social media should have the same feel and look.

As you grow your personal brand (and anyone with big goals and ambitions needs to have a personal brand, not just hide behind a company logo) it is important to establish a Facebook Page that is in your own name. That way, as you develop and grow, your Facebook Page can evolve with you. You do not know what the future holds - your life may become very different to the one you are currently living. Make sure that instead of following a brand people are following you and your work.

You will need a headshot and a banner picture. These should be in line with your branding and I recommend booking a photo shoot so that you have more than just one professional headshot.

A Facebook Page is important because from here you can create paid/sponsored ads and boosted posts. As your online skills develop, you'll create *Facebook Live* videos … achieving further reach to your audience and new audiences is crucial.

Many people I coach are resistant to using their personal Facebook profile to post about anything work-related, but this is missing a trick. Yes, you might not want to sell actively from there, but the more people who know about what you do, the better, and in the early days of starting in a new field, you probably have far more friends than page followers. Make the most of your largest pool of connections. I also encounter clients afraid of their family and friends judging what they do if they post on their personal page. If you are good at what you do and believe you deserve it, it does not matter what anyone else thinks. Refer back to the *limiting belief* and *Inner Critic* work and take stock of your thought habits surrounding posting on social media and being seen by your mum, the bully from school, your old colleagues.

Ensure that the image and name you use on your social media profiles reflects your brand and your personality. A key component of increasing your influence online within your industry is the ability to interact in other people's Facebook Groups. Your personal profile image becomes a strong piece of branding and association, so ensure you have cohesion across the board of your social media presence on various platforms.

Facebook Story is becoming more popular and works in a similar way to *Instagram Stories*, where the content disappears within 24 hours. This creates a feeling of scarcity and intimacy for those following you and is anticipated to become much more widely used in the future. You can duplicate content between these two platforms. Story content tends to be more *fly on the wall* and personal, although always give thought to your positioning. Think to yourself before you post - 'Is this *on message* and *on brand?*' Am I telling the right story to boost my credibility? Work out the best ways to spread your message and visibility across as many platforms as possible, including LinkedIn, Instagram and YouTube. It is possible to re-purpose much of your content if you are strategic about it. Consistency is key. Show up again and again, in person, sharing who you are, what you do and what you are passionate about and your connections and influence will begin to grow.

By leading with value, knowledge and expertise about the industry you are passionate about you are creating content marketing. You are giving to your audience and followers valuable information before you are asking anything from them. You are putting your insights and experience into the marketplace in order to attract the right people. People often wonder: why would I share information for free? This form of attraction marketing is about educating and giving value. Before you are anywhere near asking people to buy from you, recommending you or even creating a service or product for them to buy, let them discover for themselves all about you and what you do, and why it benefits them. You'll spread your learnings, knowledge, expertise and credibility. Carve out trust and loyalty so that the right people are drawn to you and stick around because they like you. People buy people, and the more you can show up as the real, authentic you, the more trust and authority you will build in their mind.

Love it or hate it, social media can play a big role in increasing your reach and following (and therefore your impact, influence and income!) Communicating and connecting with your audience, however big or small, is one of the fundamental rules of building a tribe. And a loyal tribe makes you more visible. Make each individual you encounter online and in person feel valued by prioritising responses to each comment and creating regular, valuable content around your areas of passion and expertise. Blogs, creative images, videos, *Facebook Lives*, even long story posts can be considered valuable content. Using different forms can quickly establish you as a leader or rising star in your field. This does not have to be overwhelming. For example, there are many ways to repurpose content. A *Facebook Live* video can be shared on Youtube or LinkedIn, or edited for a podcast episode, or turned into a blog series. People want to know 'how' and 'why' - so break down your knowledge and expertise into tiny, incremental steps that you can spread across many blog posts.

The most compelling content we consume on social media are the personal stories. The more you share about your work, your mission, your struggles (whilst positioning yourself as a being one step ahead), the more people will be attracted to you and your work. This comes as a result of the trust established through continued professionalism combined with the vulnerability you share. Now, don't get me wrong. I'm not suggesting you share everything you do. I don't share much about my children or my husband, but I share enough of my personality and interests away from business that anyone following me feels as though they know parts of my life.

Posts with photos of yourself tend to get more attention than ones you don't appear in, and much more traction that posts that just contain text or quotes. Posts containing information about you in story form are more likely to be read than scrolled past. Videos and particularly *Facebook Lives* on replay get more eyes on them than picture posts, and the current Facebook algorithms push this kind of content to more people. Effective attraction marketing is about connection, vulnerability and the story you weave about yourself as a person of influence in your field. Ultimately, if you are going to put content out into the world, you should maximise the chance of it being seen!

Break your content into easily digestible sections or ideas for longer story posts or Facebook Live content. They don't need to be sagas, just created with purpose -

always bearing in mind who you intend to attract (more on your ideal client later). Once you have begun to establish your identity on social media you'll begin adding a *Call to Action* (or CTA) on many of your posts. For example, you'll provide a link to your Facebook Group, a link to your Freebie/Opt-In/Lead Magnet, a request to share your post or blog. Gradually, you'll incorporate clear instructions to your followers/audience on how to interact with you. The more direct you are about the specific action you want readers to take, the better your responses will be.

Activity: What could I share?

Make a list of the life story events that you could share on social media posts:

Keeping up with social media can be a challenge. I made it easy for myself to be consistent, by creating a checklist that I fill in on a daily basis. Over the course of a week, I can see how many actions I have taken to get in front of my audience. You can access your own copy of the *Social Media Visiblity* Checklist here –

www.annaparkernaples.co.uk/social-media-checklist.

One realization I had when uncovering my limiting beliefs and the wounding words of my Inner Critic (me!) was that *I* was the only one responsible for creating my own success. Nobody was going to blow *my* trumpet. Nobody was going to build useful connections for me. Nobody was going to be responsible for getting the word out that I know my stuff and I'm good at it. It was a game-changer to work on myself and then to transfer this to social media. Do the work on yourself first … then focus on building and fostering your own credibility. Once you begin to do that, you'll be astonished at how quickly the results, rewards and financial returns show up in the field you are passionate about. But it all starts with you, and what's going on in your mind. If at core you are fearful of sharing your worth, then getting visible will be uncomfortable and difficult to achieve. Change how you feel about your own abilities and you can stand in your own spotlight confidently.

6

CONNECT WITH THOSE WHO NEED TO SEE YOU

Your success relies on your connection with others in your field. The saying goes that no man is an island, and in terms of getting ahead, being seen, noticed and appreciated, you cannot do that alone. Someone has to do the seeing, the noticing and the appreciating.

I missed this crucial point in my early careers. I thought I had to find success on my own, against all odds. I believed that if I pushed hard enough, for long enough, I would reach my goals. And to a certain extent, I was right. But do you recall that limiting belief I held about belonging? Well - that one kept me from building community and connection and was my undoing in my early acting career.

I was so focused on the need to prove that I was good enough ... that I stood out, that I was different, better, superior. I did not appreciate the value of connecting with my peers and as a consequence missed out on potential recommendations, referrals and social support. With hindsight and experience in other fields, I now see that the distance I created led to frustration and inability to get ahead in a busy industry.

You never know who of your peers and colleagues will become successful and an authority. You do not know the extent of their present and future connections. In my rush to get ahead, I did not cultivate relationships, rapport and friendship with others at the same stages in their career as me. This closed off potential avenues of opportunity to me simply because I did not see these individuals as worthwhile to connect with. I did not place value on those in a similar position to me. I focused my efforts exclusively on being noticed by those in positions of influence.

What I understand now, having run several businesses both online and offline, is that the relationships, collaborations and connections you nurture are invaluable. Yes, you might want bigger success than your peers … yes, you might have an inkling that you are more talented … but it is *how you make people feel* that makes a difference to how much you and your business will flourish.

I now realise that one of the most important elements of success is to widen your circle of influence, become valued in your field and create feelings of trust and liking towards you. Actually, you should be creating connections that run deeper than liking - how can you make people love you? The answer - by building relationships, trust and respect - one person at a time.

The limiting beliefs we worked through earlier in this book played a major part in my lack of connections with peers. Remember how I was scared that I would not stand out if I fitted in? Recall how at the same time I desperately wanted to be accepted, liked, trusted. I see these dual beliefs working against each other time and again in clients I work with. It holds them back since every step they take in the direction of their dreams - to stand out, to be noticed and applauded - at the same time makes them uncomfortable and afraid of further rejection.

It showed up for me like this: I would go to an audition for a part I wanted and it would start with a group workshop element. I would be a natural leader in the group - the first with my hand up, the first to volunteer. I would be pushing to prove myself, be noticed and be seen, and I did a good job of orchestrating that. But underneath, I felt that maybe I was too much, too showy, too eager. So then I would pull back, disengage, become aloof. I'd tell myself that it was obvious I did not fit in with the group and that was why I wasn't bonding easily with other auditionees in group work. One step forward, one step back. Keeping me stuck.

In my personal life I would go to parties and be fixated on how I didn't fit in. I'd opt for the quiet conversations at the edge of the room, seeking deep and meaningful conversations which made me tick, whilst at the same time wishing I was in the thick of the activity at the heart and soul of the party. Even if I had had a nice evening, I would ruminate on who hadn't spoken with me, the moments when I had felt left out, who had rejected me and why. I would focus on not belonging, which in turn meant this was how I felt when I next went to a party or social event.

It's a vicious cycle. If you don't realise that you can choose your thoughts, you accept every thought crossing your mind as fact and truth. And so – rejection becomes your truth. You have the proof that you don't fit in.

Finding out about limiting beliefs was life-changing. Accepting that there were in fact many moments at social occasions where I perpetuated my own myth that I was excluded was like a lightbulb. I came to appreciate a massive learning: If I am on the lookout for rejection, I am not paying attention to the inclusive smiles, the moments of connection with others, the decision I have taken to hang back, my body language, my emotions, my feelings as I enter a room. Behind my thoughts and actions lay this fear of rejection and not belonging. In terms of networking, forget it. Yes, I would be able to stride in confidently and make a show of telling people about what I did … but inside I focused on how I wasn't any good at building connections because I never fit in! It's interesting that I doubt anyone would have known how I felt, how I was seeing the world. And yet I'd imagine that my confident exterior did not belie my self-doubt. This prevented me from focusing on the other person and so I could not establish rapport, essential for building relationships and connection. I was too locked in my own rejection story and the need to prove myself.

Once the *I do not belong* thought was reprogrammed through limiting belief work and NLP exercises, I found for the first time that I could relax socially. I could also forge ahead in my career. I could take risks - show up and be seen - because I knew I was responsible for cultivating my own sense of inclusion. I'd been deleting the other two million pieces of information per second at every social engagement that indicated that I was respected, loved, valued. I simply did not see those possibilities, because my mind was attuned to rejection.

As I write this I realise it sounds utterly loopy. And that's the point. We are so engrossed by our thoughts that we believe every one of them. But they are not the only truth. There are myriad ways we can interpret any given situation.

With this knowledge my real confidence grew. Not the *I'm putting my armour on* and *going out to fight the world* type confidence that presents a show to the world of strength but is actually deeply isolating … but confidence in who I am and how I choose to interact with the world around me. I don't have to be offended if I don't hit it off with someone. It doesn't mean that I'm not liked or that they are judging me. They could be having a zillion and one thoughts in their head, none of which are really about me. They are busy looking at the world through their own unique model and interpretation of events, and most likely are more concerned with whether they are good enough themselves!

Personal responsibility

With the awareness that I can take responsibility to build rapport and relationships, and an understanding that it is just as easy to believe that I belong as it is to believe that I don't, my professional and social connections transformed.

Through the exercise I shared earlier where I examined my core limiting beliefs, I knew for the first time that I had a choice in how I think about myself. It was not a universally accepted truth that I did not belong. I had perpetuated that belief and raked over my experiences to find the proof. What would happen if I changed that part of my story? What would happen if I chose instead to belong, to seek out connection, relationship and mutual respect amongst my peers?

I decided that it would serve me better to believe that wherever I go, I am accepted and that I belong. And this gave me the power to choose where **I wanted** to belong. Was I spending my time and attention on people who were not actually who I wanted to surround myself with? Did other people's opinions of me matter? No, not really.

I can choose my responses to comments and interactions. And I can cultivate relationships that I do want to have. For the first time, I felt I had choice.

At this point my work was focused on voice acting, specifically audiobook narration. If I was going to belong anywhere, I wanted to belong with those of influence at the fore of that industry. Research showed that many of these individuals were based in the US.

I booked a flight to New York, to attend an event where I knew absolutely no-one. All of the key decision-makers that I wanted to meet would likely be in the same room at a prestigious awards event. I flew 3500 miles to go and meet with CEO's, casting directors, agents and leading international publishers who did not know me from Adam.

Was I nervous? Yes. Did I find it easy to walk in and make connections? At first, no. But then I reminded myself that essentially everybody wants to belong, to feel important, valued and special, and that I could cultivate relationships in the room that way. I reminded myself that I had just as much right to be in that room, amongst industry experts, as anybody else. I was passionate about the niche field, I knew myself to be talented, capable and able and I knew I was ready to belong wherever I chose. I chose to belong at the top of the industry.

The results of that evening were staggering. I made so many important connections because I walked tall, comfortably and confidently as I talked about my experience, plans and abilities. I made some fast acquaintances, some of which have become friends. Chiefly, though, I began some interactions that led to me landing a $30,000 contract by 9.00 the next morning.

If I had continued to believe I could not belong in that industry, I would never have risked buying the ticket to fly to that event. If I had focused on being a fraud, or too inexperienced, I would never have had the courage to walk into that prestigious awards gala event on my own. It was a pivotal moment in my career. And in my confidence. I now had proof that a sense of belonging FIRST was paramount to my results.

In whatever area I work, I now make it a core part of my mission to connect with both peers and industry leaders. I find ways to collaborate. I find ways to help others gain recognition, without the nagging fear that they will overtake me. Instead I applaud and celebrate the success of others. *Their* success does not correspond to *my* failure. There is room for all. Helping others to have a metaphorical boost over the fence doesn't mean I am left stranded behind.

A new concept began to form in my mind - *collaboration is better than competition*. The scarcity mindset had driven many of my behaviours before – a belief that I had to push, push, push to get noticed. It was now dawning on me that helping lift up my fellow man creates good feeling amongst colleagues and industry peers. By helping someone else out through recommendations, referrals and introductions, I could induce the desire to help me out reciprocally. Help didn't necessarily come immediately, and it was not always of the same type or size that I had given, but there was a definite increase in the leads and potential connections that came my way over the next 12 months or so since I consciously went out of my way to help others to up-level. I became *valuable* and *valued*. It had the added benefit of giving me purpose in my networking. Instead of thinking solely, 'What can I get from this event?' I was concentrating on how I might refer business someone else's way. The relationships I built were much more connected, right from the word go. Instead of thinking about what I wanted to say next, I was really listening, paying attention to what the other person needed for their own success.

Leading with giving value is now a fundamental part of how I run my business. I want to give as much as I can, for free, no strings attached, as often as possible. The old version of me would have thought this was nuts, that I was crazy for 'giving it all away' with no thanks or payment. The new me could now see how effective this was as a long-term strategy. Connections matter. How you make people feel matters. Connection, trust and community are the cornerstone of any business success.

Connection counts

In this chapter, we're going to look at ways you can begin to form connections with other people in order to establish your own credibility, authority and status. But first off, what is it to *connect?* The dictionary tells us that it is to: *Form a relationship or feel an affinity … Join together so as to provide access and communication … Bring together or into contact so that a real or notional link is established.* Connection is valuable for positioning *you* in your field. Bringing people together and getting out and meeting new people increases trust, likability and loyalty from those you enable to connect with others. It is a powerful way to assert your validity and expertise.

As human beings, we remember how others make us feel and we recall easily when people have connected us with others in the same boat as us, or even when we have been introduced to someone we perceive as more influential. We remember with good feeling the people who have helped to lift us.

Bringing others together who share similar wants, needs and interests is one of the best ways to develop your business in its early stages. Developing connection and community provides you with options for easy marketing opportunities and an increase in sales and bookings. It elevates your status in other people's eyes, raises your kudos and creates trust. Over time, you'll see an increase in referrals, recommendations and followers as a result of consistency in nurturing your connections.

So how do you build connection when you are just getting started, or have been going in your business venture for a while and don't feel as though you have many contacts? We're going to look at how you foster a sense of community, build on trust and give value both online (with particular attention to Facebook Groups) and in person at networking events. Whilst, at first, harnessing your networks may seem time-consuming and hard work for little immediate return, it will become one of the most valuable activities for your business, and is worth doing right from the start.

How can I connect?

Before we begin looking at how you can connect with other people, let's explore how you describe what you do and why you do it. If you're going to be connecting and networking with people, you should ensure they under-stand how they can best serve you too, if they choose to at a later date. Introducing yourself in person and online in a succinct, clear way establishes not only your expertise, leadership and strengths but crucially who you can help and why they need you.

Once you have the foundation for what you want to say about yourself, you'll be able to use it both formally and informally, adjusting it for the setting and situation. A *pitch* is a means of introducing yourself and the value of your work either in person or online. In the next section I'll show you how to create a formal pitch, an informal pitch and carry over the insights from this work to your online profiles and media presence.

The pitch

A formal business pitch is a presentation by one or more people to an investor or group of investors, though it can also be an email, letter, or even an impromptu conversation. It is a way of introducing yourself and the basic concepts of your business, where you fit, your ideal customers and the authority or influence you already have. In a formal pitch, the purpose is to request money to build your business. The *call to action* is an important part of discussing your business and the more you become accustomed to asking for help, be it referrals, investment, requests to follow links or to follow on social media, the better results you will get.

Most likely you'll be using a pitch informally, however, a basic understanding of how a pitch structure works will stand you in good stead for when you get out networking in person more often.

It is useful to have a one minute pitch (approx.150 words) for networking situations and a three minute pitch (approx.450 words) for when those more formal occasions arise, plus a 30 second version (about 75 words) that you might use as an intro on your *Facebook Lives* or when someone asks what you do in a casual setting. The more you speak about what you do and why, the more fluid your delivery, which will in turn begin to carry more authority and credibility.

There is a basic structure to follow for creating a pitch. You won't need to include all of these elements when you speak informally, but having a grasp of what they are and how they can be used is useful:

Your Hook

This is the opener of a formal pitch. It is a way to grab people's attention with a fact or a story headline. It could be a question, a personal moment of realisation about what you do, a statistic or some other human element that you can discuss.

Effective openers I recall are: a female empowerment coach specialising in anxiety shared statistics around teenage girls' self-harm rates. It made everyone in the room sit up and pay attention; a worker from a modern-day slavery charity introduced her business with the number of modern-day slaves that had likely been involved in bringing to that room the gadgets and tech and clothing that we take for granted. I often share my journey from wheelchair to Hollywood.

Activity: How could you grab attention?

What could you say about what you do that would grab attention? Jot some ideas below:

The Problem or Pain you solve

This is the part where you begin to reveal the issues you are trying to solve through your business offering:

What is the scale of this problem?

Why should people care about the problem that you are fixing?

How many people are affected?

How deeply are they affected by the problem?

Make sure you keep this part super-simple and use jargon a five-year-old would understand. This part should be understood by those both in and out of your industry as this is how people will remember you when they encounter someone with the specific problem that you solve. For my coaching business, I talk about the fears entrepreneurs have that prevent them from scaling. I talk about how this affects their household income and their sense of fulfilment.

Activity: What is the problem?

What problem are you trying to solve for other people? Why is this an issue?

Your Solution

This is where you position your value and uniqueness. For me, it's an opportunity to talk about the results people get from working with me and my services - increased confidence, increased income, increased potential impact on their communities. In terms of uniqueness, I talk of my own successes in becoming visible, how I have been in both a place of dissatisfaction and achievement as a result of the strategic work I provide. I am living proof.

Activity: What is the answer?

What solution are you providing to the specific problem you already mentioned?

What is unique about what you do?

What makes it a game-changer for people to invest in?

How is it different to other services/products out there?

Your Revenue Model

This is where you share the specific HOW of what your business does, the services and products you provide. In my case, my revenue model includes membership, group programmes, private coaching, masterminds, books, audios and my podcast. You don't have to discuss the level of pricing, just indicate the ways in which you get the results and the ways clients and customers can pay you.

Activity: The money

How do you make money doing what you do?

Do you offer a variety of services and products?

What revenue streams do you have/plan to have to help your customers with this problem?

Your Competition or Risk awareness

Sharing an understanding of who else is in your field is useful for elevating your own status and for providing an immediate understanding of to whom your service might be of most benefit. Business owners often worry that by talking about their competitors they put themselves at risk. It is often quite the contrary. By sharing this knowledge you position yourself strongly.

Activity: The competition

Who are your competitors?

What do you do differently?

How will stand out/compete with them?

Your Team

This is where you demonstrate the strength of the people you work with. Even if you work on your own or use only the occasional outsourcer, it is worth considering the value of your wider connections. If you have skilled employees or an exceptionally strong network of followers it's worth shouting about them.

Activity: Who do you work with?

Who is in your team/community/wider connections?

What are their skills and experience?

Which mentors, coaches and advisors impact your work?

What does your future team look like?

How are you looking to grow or outsource?

Your Traction so far

This is where you demonstrate the progress and success you have had to date. You can talk about how established you are as a business, and the level of understanding you have around your customers' needs. This section gives you an opportunity to show off a little, to share accolades, press and publicity and is where you can share valuable endorsements and results.

Activity: What do I bring?

What have you done in terms of sales, research, getting customers and processing orders?

What market research have you done?

What press coverage, endorsements or awards have you had?

What do you need to do to build credibility?

Your Ask

Get in the habit right from the start of always giving a *Call to Action* (CTA) after introducing yourself online or in person. The more specific and direct you can be with how someone else can help you, the better your results. If you want feedback, ask for it. Want a specific type of contact? Shares of your page or videos online? Referrals? Be as clear as possible in order to boost your chances of getting the action you desire.

Activity: What do I want them to do?

What action should the person you are speaking to take right now?

What do you need today that will progress your business?

Who do you most want to be connected with?

Activity: Write those pitches

Use the information you've jotted in each of the above sections to compile three different pitches - 450 words, 150 words and 75 words.

Script them, say them out loud and refine any sections that don't flow. Get really comfortable with saying what you do and who you help so that when the time comes to say your piece in real life, it is easy. You know what to say and how to say it … this enables you to come across, and feel, much more confident when you say it, which in turn establishes trust in your abilities to do what you say you do! One top tip from my years as a performer is to record the script out loud onto your phone and then listen to it over and over whilst doing other activities such as walking, driving or the washing up. For some reason, it seems to go into the brain much more easily. Remember - you don't need to be word perfect but you do want to be concise and memorable. I find that once I know the basic structure of my pitch, I can add in or take away elements depending on where I am and who I am speaking with. Creating a pitch and understanding how to communicate what you do adds a level of confidence in how you discuss your work, particularly useful in casual conversations about what you do for a living. Countless times I've heard people say that they find it awkward telling people in social situations what they do. To me, that's a shame. Everyone we come into contact with has at least 200-300 people that they are in regular contact with and if you convey your message clearly, you never know when they might just be in a position to recommend you and what you do. If you are too embarrassed to share your value, how you can you expect the results you want? Invest time doing this exercise thoroughly … make the words feel easy and natural through repetition and through using simple language and you will give yourself the best chance to impress on others the value of the solution you offer.

Your ideal client

Before we move on to how to build more connections, it's important to work out exactly who you want to work with. Having a specific ideal client model does not mean you won't attract or work with anyone else. What it does mean is that you can niche down in the words you use and the marketing you do because you have a greater appreciation of the pain or problem they are struggling with. Or it might not be a problem they have ... it might be more that you create a *gain* for them, that you offer something positive to their life. We're going to look at who your ideal client might be and the value that you bring to them. This will give a clearer picture of the words and language that will attract them in your social media posts, marketing, emails and website copy.

Activity: Your niche

What is the problem you have identified that you and your service can help with?

Who has the problem or need that you have identified?

How big is the problem or need for that customer?

How does it affect their everyday life?

How many people face this problem?

What do your ideal clients have in common? (Gender, age, marital status, children, income, country, religion, background, occupation, beliefs, etc.) Give as much detail as possible - this exercise is so worthwhile.

For each type of person that might have the problem, drill down further. Give them a name, age, marital status, family life. How educated are they? What do they do for fun? What is going on in their lives that matters to them? This is called an Ideal Client avatar and once you are clearer on each avatar, it'll become so much easier to target them in all of your advertising and interactions.

Think about the following:

Are they prepared to pay to change the situation?

How much are they able to pay?

What is the transformation worth to them?

One of the biggest issues I discovered when launching my first online business was that I had completed insufficient market research to test whether my assumptions were true. Ok, I'll admit I did practically none. I didn't have a clue how to go about doing it! I just assumed that because I thought my idea was a good one that others would too. I invested hours and money creating a membership service without ascertaining whether enough people who fitted my ideal client brief would value my membership enough to pay. I would hear again and again that people thought it was a great idea, but that they didn't want to pay for it, or have sufficient funds to do so. As a result - once you have an idea of your ideal client I urge you to evaluate your answers by finding from those exact people whether they want what you plan to offer. Are you creating an offer based solely on your own needs, without stopping to work out if it is viable as a business service? Ask yourself:

How can I know if my assumptions about what my ideal client wants are true?

Do I know for sure that these problems exist or do I need to test my assumptions?

If you discover that you're making some unresearched assumptions, turn to social media to get the answers you need. It's easy to use the search box for terms that might apply to your potential clients and join Facebook groups where your ideal clients are likely to be and become an active participant in conversations. Run polls and ask questions around pain points. You can even set up surveys or run online quizzes to get the answers you need. Look out for the kinds of words people use when they answer your questions. Better still, if you can get people on a call (perhaps in return for a free consultation or something of value to them) you can really listen closely to how they describe their pain points and how the difficulty they are encountering affects them. This is like gold dust for you – you can sprinkle your posts and emails with the words and phrases you hear.

Activity: Find out about the client

What Facebook Groups could you visit to find out if your beliefs are true?

What research do you need to do?

What feelings does your ideal client have about their problem?

What outcome do they want?

What desire do you help them fulfil?

What feelings do you help them to have?

How big is this pain point for your ideal client?

Is what you offer 'life and death' or 'nice to have'?

*Is your business a **pain reliever** or a **gain creator** or both?*

What value do you add to your client?

What will your client be able to do as a result of your product or service?

I know this chapter has included a lot of work digging down for exactly what you offer, your pitch and your ideal clients, and I promise you that this work will form the basis of all your online marketing, your professional connections and the core of how you promote yourself. People buy because they identify with the pain points you talk about and want the result you offer. They will choose you because of your consistency, authenticity and the personal story you share that resonates with what they are experiencing.

Go back and review the work we did around your own life story. Now that you have a greater understanding of your ideal client, what parts of your story will appeal? Sharing your journey helps to establish a feeling of 'likeness'. We like to be around people that are the same as us. We like to feel as though we belong. No matter what your business service is, sharing your story, shaped for effect on your ideal client, is a powerful way to draw the right people to you. By being clear about who you want to attract, you will naturally repel those who don't get you and what you are about. And that is more than OK. Not everyone will 'get' you. They don't have to. You are only interested in harnessing those that do connect with your message.

Challenge yourself to create at least one social media post each day this week that shares a part of your story, includes part of your pitch and offers a call to action such as 'click this link', 'send me a message' or 'comment below'. The more you get into the habit of giving direct requests, the sooner you teach your audience to take specific action. Become aware of posts you enjoy reading on social media. How often are you drawn to posts that reveal something of the person sharing the content? To be clear, I'm not suggesting you bare all. You can talk about past experiences or present frustrations without dealing the whole deck. Always remember that the point about posting is not about YOU. It is about your ideal client - on every post. Ask yourself before sharing a picture of your dinner with the world if it is of value to your ideal client. If it is, then fine - share your salad or smoothie for all to see. But if it isn't, either craft the post so that it will resonate with them or don't post at all. Every interaction you have on social media is a building block in creating your personal brand. Make sure you are laying the right foundations to draw the right people to you.

Becoming a connector of others is powerful. If you put yourself at the heart of a community that shares the same desires and pain points, and, through consistency and rapport-building, position yourself as an expert or leader whilst at the same time remaining approachable, you will be well on your way to creating relationships with potential buyers, loyal customers and raving fans!

Build and lead a community

Establishing a Facebook Group is a fantastic (and free) way to stamp out your authority and to bring people together in a community. People have a need to belong and this is a simple way to engage that desire for connection. Did a sense of isolation or loneliness come up for your ideal client? It's worth thinking about the value of belonging as this will be a prime incentive for working with you and participating in your group.

When I suggest establishing a Facebook Group to my clients there are some common objections. These include the worry that you'll become merely an administrator, or that running a group is a lot of work for no return. I'd counter those fears by telling you that rather than being an administrator at the beck and call of your members, you are the leader, connecter and authority within that group. You set the rules and you don't have to take any rubbish from anyone - you are in control. Running a Facebook Group can be time consuming, however, it is the best way to gain respect and regular awareness of you and what you do. So that time is well invested. Yes, it can take a while to get interaction to flow but with consistency and determination you can create a thriving tribe of your own. What is exciting about a Facebook Group is that even when there is not much engagement or interaction, it is still a valuable way to bring in new clients. Interestingly, in my own Facebook Groups I can have many 'silent' watchers who neither comment nor post, but will message me privately, buy my courses or products and open all my emails. You never know who is watching and what they are thinking. Just because a Facebook Group does not flow with chatter without your input does not mean it isn't serving its purpose - to build your authority and be a source of warm leads for your business.

As I mentioned earlier, current estimates are that it takes 22-32 touch points before someone notices you and what you do. It used to be around seven touch points before a sale in the days before social media. Whilst the idea of creating 22 pieces of content before being noticed might to some seem overwhelming, to me it is exciting. A Facebook Group gives you an increased chance of your posts being seen – current Facebook algorithms favour community. You can carry on posting about what you do and how you serve, understanding that most people don't even consciously take onboard what you are saying. Yet.

You do not need a huge group to be highly profitable, either. Even as few as 30-50 members who are engaged and reading your posts will form the foundations of a thriving business when it comes to converting to paying clients and customers.

When creating your Facebook Group the name you give it can make a big difference to how searchable it is and how easy it is to understand who it is for. The name doesn't have to be set in stone. Whilst you have under 5000 members you can change the name of your group if you wish to down the line. You should ensure, however, that your ideal client knows it is right for them just by its title. Give some thought to the desires, pain points and identity of your ideal client. Give thought also to whether you intend to have a group for all in your industry including your peers, the people who look up to you and potentially the more experienced/established leaders in your field, or whether to keep it exclusively to those who might purchase your goods or services.

Activity: Your group

Who is your Facebook Group for?

Who is it not for?

What is the purpose of the Group?

Why should people join?

Make a list of some suitable Facebook Group name ideas:

As a minimum, to set up your Facebook Group, you will need the group name, a brief description - including its purpose and aims - a bit about you and a cover picture.

Consider creating a rule around self-promotion within your group. This will set the boundaries for participation and will make your administration duties much easier from the outset. You will also need to create an image for the group banner picture. Using an image of yourself within the banner would establish your authority and ownership of the space and can be created using a template in the right size from a photo editing app such as Canva or PicMonkey.

Set some short questions for when people join. You can use one of the questions to build your email list by offering an incentive for giving an email address such as a freebie - opt-in or giveaway - some kind of ethical bribe where you give something of value to the requester to download in exchange for their highly coveted email address. I often give away some valuable content - a useful checklist or information guide, or even a hypnosis audio - so that there is a specific reason and desire to join my mailing list. Hint – no one wants to join your newsletter, not really. They'll only do it if there is something good in it for them. Other questions I have asked at this stage in joining my group have aimed to get specific information around pain points or even how they found my group. This tells me which marketing strategies are effective in terms of building my group and I can redouble my efforts in that area. I pop everything I have learned into a spreadsheet and then accept the new member into my group. The information is lost to you once you click 'accept' so I'd definitely advise not being too hasty to let them in!

Activity: Good questions for member requests

Write some ideas for other questions to ask potential members:

Before you announce your new group, create some scheduled posts to go out throughout the week. Consider what topics, questions, polls might be of interest. What ideas could you use for regular posts? For example, could Monday be 'Self-promotion' day? Could Friday be 'Share a quote' day? Think about what you can put out there on a regular basis for maximum engagement.

Create a welcome post and tag every new member in it to encourage interaction and expectations from the start. Remember, it may seem like hard work to grow your group in the beginning, but it is a brilliant way to remind people about what you do and the value you can bring to them. Plan into your week some dedicated time for building connections on and offline, both in your own group and in others. Visit the Facebook Groups where your ideal client is likely to be spending time and begin to post value. There may be opportunities to share your group link or invite people to your group. Lead with value in all of your interactions online and make this a non-negotiable part of running your business. Through consistency and targeted activity, you will begin to grow your own tribe.

Real-life networking

I've talked a lot in this chapter about online networking and harnessing connection on Facebook particularly. Don't forget, though, that networking IN REAL LIFE makes a big difference in the way you build connections and awareness of your work. If you want to become THE go-to person in your industry, look out for local networking events. Try a few as a guest before deciding which to attend regularly. Without a doubt, the best results from networking come through consistency and showing up (so not dissimilar to your online actions). The main thing is to know that you are there to spread the word on what you do, but primarily to go with the aim of connecting with and helping other people. This is the key to being remembered and valued within a networking community. It is not about the individuals you meet there but having contact with the hundreds of people in their world, too. It is possible to go to an event and think, 'These aren't the right kind of people,' but don't worry. It is not been a waste of your time. You never know who they'll be sitting next to at dinner one day. If you can clearly communicate who you help and how, it may just be your name and service that gets recommended.

When attending networking events, brush up on your pitch and be clear on a suitable 'ask', both informally and in more formal introduction sessions. That way you can ensure your time is productive. Know why you are going and who you hope to be introduced to.

Activity: Networking

Make a list of local networking events, dates and times:

Make a list of industry-related networking events:

Events on a national level may be planned many months in advance. Research possible networking events for your industry and diarise them now.

In-person networking can be a challenge. Remember that what you do, the service you provide and the meaning behind your product are more important than your fear! Go back and look at the work around your Inner Critic. What are you afraid of? Is it Imposter Syndrome? The fear that you will be found out for not being as good at what you do as they say you are? This Inner Critic chatter is not helpful (nor true). If you find yourself shying away from networking in person, I urge you to do further work on your limiting beliefs. It could transform everything for you in terms of the community you create, the connections you build, the financial success you can have as a result of showing up as someone who is good at what they do and deserves to get the results that they do. Confidence and self-assuredness do not have to be arrogant. Confidence in your abilities instils trust, so make sure you remind people of what you can do.

Becoming a connector of people can increase your authority, which we'll look at in more detail in the next chapter. Look at your interactions now and ask 'How can I add more value?' 'How can I position my expertise?' Perhaps more importantly, ask yourself how you can be of service to others, connect them with the information and people that they should be in touch with. These simple actions will transform your business and personal brand ... people will feel positive about their interactions with you. *You* are your brand, wherever you go and whatever you do.

7

YOU ARE THE AUTHOR OF YOUR AUTHORITY

Become a recognised leader in your field and clients will come flocking. The key to your business success and being the go-to person in your industry is elevating your status. Take a look at the field you are in. There are probably a few people who spring to mind when you think about those who are really nailing what they do. These are the people who are well-connected, respected, their names on everyone's lips for recommendations. It is no accident that they are seen as being at the top or the best in your niche area of business. They are not there solely because their talents are strides above the rest. They may well be talented, capable individuals, full of raw charisma and exceptional knowledge. However, it is not those qualities that has led to them being noticed and remembered.

The first time I experienced a meteoric rise in my success (connections, referrals, reputation preceding me) was after I had begun my formal training in NLP. As you already know, the effect of changing my language had impacted my health, my confidence, pretty much everything about how I saw myself. Once I noticed the level of success I had achieved in voiceovers I decided that I wanted to niche even further - by specialising in audiobook work. But this was not enough and I knew that drilling down into exactly how I wanted to position myself would make all the difference. I crafted myself as the go-to British female teen voice for Young Adult Fiction. In the US, audiobooks were a rapidly growing field with a level of prestige attached to the narrator and was comparatively well-paid for top narrators, whilst in the UK it was considered more as something 'proper' actors did when they couldn't get any other work, poorly paid and inflexible. In the States, studios had moved with the times to allow narrators to work remotely, understanding that technology had improved and quality could still be assured. In the UK it was considered sub-standard to record remotely. I knew that cracking the US market would work for me as it ticked all of my boxes - I could work from home and do the school runs, create audio from my home studio and send it across the Atlantic by the wonders of technology. I could work on creative projects, sharing stories that impact lives. I could perform the nuances of emotion that the various characters experienced. I also knew that if I created the right connections, I could be celebrated for my work, and I knew that I would be paid well for my efforts.

I set out to position myself amongst the best. I sought out those with much experience and I followed their work, their online activities. I connected with them. I joined Facebook Groups and shared value. I shared blogs on the journey of my work. I shared insights into the trials and tribulations of the niche we were in. I became consistent in my efforts to connect with those on a similar journey to me, and those who were much more experienced. I asked advice, I gave advice. I reminded people over and over about my niche style, as THE young female British narrator. When you feel connected and seek out others with the same passion as you, it is uplifting. I found over time that I would be asked for my opinion, that I would be asked to speak on panels in the UK and the US. This happened because I was clear about what I was good at and where I was going. I was clear about which producers and publishers I could help and how, and I was specific about where I wanted to position myself from the start - at the top. I wanted to aim for the high-paying, prestigious bookings and be amongst the best in the business. Can you recall the image I shared with you at the beginning of this book of me standing on the red carpet in Hollywood for the seventh award? It was an award for a co-narrated title and I was the only female amongst seven other narrators, all of them male, all of them revered in the industry. I had deliberately created relationships and connections with other individuals of influence and that had a direct impact on the level of standing and kudos I attained. I had watched the activities and behaviours of those with influence and created my own version of that. Opportunities and connections I previously never dreamed of came easily because I had raised my profile with consistent action and attention.

When I decided to change my focus and use what I had learned through NLP to teach people about the power of mindset, I used the same techniques to get visible and connected quickly. I modelled those already successful in areas of motivational speaking and in coaching and created my own version of those behaviours. Within eight months of consistent action I had spoken on stages alongside household names such as Ruby Wax, Will Young and Paul McKenna. I had been featured in leading online and print publications, such as *Psychologies Magazine, Happiful Magazine, Breathe* and *Kindred Spirit.* I'd appeared on radio, podcasts and in high-profile blogs. And I was nominated for an *Inspiration Award for Women* for my work to inspire people to change their lives, winning alongside fellow award-winners Rio Ferdinand, Adele and Holly Willoughby in a room full of celebrities and household names. I achieved this because I was strategic in building my visibility, credibility and authority. The good news is - you, too, can replicate behaviours of excellence in your own industry to increase your impact, just like I have, over and over.

I'm not suggesting you go and copy everything an individual you admire in your industry is doing. I'm asking you to look at the actions, behaviours and interactions they have and to model your own version of those activities. It is akin to working out the routes they have taken on their journey to get them to the level they are at, and then creating your own map to get you to a similar destination. The quickest way to get success is to follow a proven pathway, and that's what I'm going to encourage you to work out.

Modelling behaviours

This chapter is all about standing out from the crowd to ensure that you build even more on the credibility, authority and connections you have begun to establish. Getting to a point where you have recognition and kudos in your industry is a process, not luck. By the end of this chapter you'll have a better understanding of the practical steps you can take to make that 'magic' happen.

Modelling someone else's behaviours is one of the quickest ways to work out how to get ahead and get noticed. Modelling behaviours does not mean copying, it is more like following a recipe and adding in your own twist. In whatever industry you are in, there will be people you admire, respect and perhaps even envy a little for the successes they have achieved. Maybe these individuals are more successful than you … maybe they are only a step or two from where you are right now.

We're going to be doing some in-depth stalking (and I

don't mean the kind you can get arrested for!) By researching the behaviours, activities and connections that someone you admire in your field has taken in the past, you can get a handle on what actions and behaviours are open to you to duplicate and re-model in your own way.

Create profiles of people in your industry. You are not, I repeat NOT, intending to copy what they do, just observe and take on board the actions that have led them to where they are now.

In Neuro-Linguistic Programming (NLP), modelling is the process of recreating and replicating excellence. We can model any human behaviour by mastering the beliefs, physiology and specific thought processes that underlie the skill or behaviour that outwardly we see as successful. We can't know exactly what someone was thinking when they carried out a particular action, but we can put ourselves inside their shoes and work out our own version of events. This process is about studying how someone else goes about getting the success they strive for. It's a question of watching, working out what they do, learning how to do it and then doing it for yourself.

Activity: Modelling excellence

Pick three people you see as successful and begin to study their actions online - on social media, on their website, on a full Google search.

On social media, go back a couple of years and work out what events they attended, who they connected with, what platforms they spoke on - and see if you can connect the dots to see how they reached where they are now. Fill in the Visibility Profiles below and be really specific with your findings. Incidentally, this is also a really powerful exercise to do on your competitors:

VISIBILITY PROFILE

Name:

Job Title:

Website:

Key branding colours and style on website:

Which are their preferred social media accounts?

What events have they attended?

What events have they spoken at?

What awards have they won?

What qualifications do they hold?

Who are they mostly connecting with online?

What can you notice about their blog?

How do they make it clear what they specialise in?

Who do they collaborate with/surround themselves with?

How long have they been doing what they currently do?

How do they behave online? How consistent are they?

What are they NOT doing that you could do?

What are they doing that you could do?

Biggest learnings from researching them:

_____

Now that you have these profiles, think about what they have in common. It is most likely the authority they carry, the influence they have built within your industry and the weight that their name now carries. We're going to be getting to grips with how you can establish your own authority in your industry.

Let's start with asking, 'What is *authority*?' The Oxford English Dictionary tells us: "the power to influence others, especially because of one's commanding manner or one's recognised knowledge about something", or, "a person with extensive or specialised knowledge about a subject; an expert."

Hopefully, by now you will have a greater under-standing of the power of words and language. Not everyone relates to the terms *leader*, *expert* or *authority*, and whilst there is a whole host of work on limiting beliefs to do around your reticence to label yourself that way, it's important to know if those terms block you. Have a look at this list of synonyms for the word *authority* and note any that appeal to you more.

influence, sway, control, leverage, power, command, weight, repu-tation, standing, kudos, status, stature, prestige, gravitas, image, esteem, supremacy, superiority, eminence, rank, position, station, cred-ibility, plausibility, integrity, acceptance, trust, faith, confidence, clout, pull, professional.

If you want to have more influence, more impact and more income, gaining kudos is vital. You can cultivate your authority through regularly sharing your credibility (in your social media posts), crafting interesting articles and blog pieces, connecting with industry leaders and peers and working with collaborators. When you have this *authority* part-nailed, more opportunities, referrals and connections will come your way. You'll be better-connected and your status level will have increased amongst those following you (since you'll be sharing every single win, no matter how small, with them, day in, day out).

By building into your daily work life a commitment to look for new contacts and potential opportunities, you will begin to gain traction in crafting yourself as an authority figure. Find ways that you can be of value to those with more experience than you, and how you can bring your own expertise and knowledge to those who are less experienced. REMEMBER - you do not have to know everything to be an expert. You need only be one or two steps ahead of those who don't yet know what you know in order to be of value to them. No one knows everything, so trust that what you know is enough and that when you don't know about a particular area, trust that you can find the best person to ask.

If you ever hear people say that you should take time to work *on* your business not *in* your business, they are most likely referring to the importance of up-levelling through creating deliberate, strategic connections.

Tasks

The following prompts are going to be tasks to undertake over the coming weeks and months. I cannot stress enough how focusing on building your contacts, connections and value within your 'marketplace' will bring financial and professional dividends to you and your business.

Take a look in your diary and create a regular slot where you will spend a minimum of 30 minutes taking action to build your opportunities. The more routinely you can do this, the quicker you will see results. Make these segments of time non-negotiable.

With social media, you have in the palm of your hand the ability to build connection and establish authority with the people who want the information, knowledge and experience that you have. Authority comes from sharing value and knowledge with the people with whom you wish to engage. It is about showing your insights and experience and giving your unique slant on the content. There may be many others in your field, but nobody interprets the content exactly the way you do.

Earlier on in this book you were encouraged to compile a list of Facebook Groups that your ideal client might be found participating in. These are the perfect places to start sharing your knowledge and tips. However, as you have no doubt encountered, Facebook Groups may have their own rules and regulations and it's worth getting your head around these early on.

Explore each of the Facebook Groups you have found and write down what kind of posts you are allowed to share and when. When starting out with using groups strategically it is best to work on a maximum of five groups at a time so that you can establish yourself as a valuable group member first, before moving on to the next. New groups pop up all the time, so do a new search every month or so.

Take some time to explore the most recent posts and comments in each group. List the topics and subjects that come up again and again. These can be insightful into the concerns of the people you are trying to attract so use this information for your own benefit. Consider how could you offer value - what experience have you had with dealing with this subject that you could offer to this audience? When networking online in other Facebook Groups it's important to lead with value rather than self-promotion, unlike designated posts where you are specifically invited to share your URL links and social media handles. Get into the routine of commenting on people's posts with useful responses, always positioning yourself as a go-to person with experience. One of the best ways to do this is to make video content, especially *Facebook Lives* or podcast episodes around topics that come up again and again. That way you only have to share the value and your expertise once and make maximum impact with your knowledge.

Blogging for authority

A great way to build kudos is through writing regular content on your own blog, providing you do it strategically and follow through with a plan to share it with your audience. Blogs are useful for creating and sustaining good SEO (Search Engine Optimisation), which is turn makes you stand out from the crowd when someone looks for you on Google. Most websites have an option for blogging, so if you have an established website, use that. If you don't yet have a suitable website (and they really don't have to be complicated to create) with blogging as an option, have a look at blog-publishing sites such as Blogger. My preference is Wordpress and my websites are hosted on Wordpress, too. You can buy templates such as *Divi* and *Thrive Themes* which allow you to drag and drop the design of your website and blog and are super-simple. When beginning your blogposts, think about the title of your post. The strongest titles are those that address one of your ideal client's pain points, or mimic what someone might search for in Google if they were looking for someone like you to help them. Write your blog content in a natural, authentic voice, as you do for your social media posts. In fact, many of your longer story-style posts on social media could be easily re-purposed into blogposts.

Activity: Consider the following:

How do you want to come across in your blog? (As adventurer, a professional, down-to-earth, chatty, authoritative?)

How often will you publish a blog?

List some ideas for blogpost titles (you can schedule blog posts in advance, so you could bulk create in one go, several months ahead of time):

A good blog has the following elements:
- It tells you what it is going to tell you
- It gives you the nub of the topic
- It tells you what it just told you!
- It ends with a call to action – what to do next - share, like, sign up, download?

An easy way to get wider exposure for your blog (and **YOU** as the author!) is to 'piggyback' off other people's blogposts or content. That is, you write to review, comment on, or share someone else's ideas. The reason this is effective is that it means you can tag them in on it both online and on social media. The chances are they will be pleased to be included, to be seen as an authority and 1) share it, 2) remember that you wrote it, making you a useful connection. People remember those who support them and show up over and over again.

Field leaders

Activity: Who leads?

Who are the leaders within your field?

Make a list of books relevant to your field, and their authors:

Who runs courses on your subject?

What are the courses called? (These might give you ideas on blogpost titles):

What are the most popular magazines or publications in your field?

Who are the editors?

What are the most popular blogs in your specialty area and who writes them?

What are the smaller, up-and-coming blogs in your industry? Written by whom?

What are the products or software that may be relevant in your community?

Who makes them or sells them?

What services do you use in your own business that you can talk about?

For each of the questions you've just answered there is at least one possibility for a 'comment' blogpost - something that you found thought-provoking, interesting, controversial. By including industry leaders and those only a few steps ahead of you in your blog posts you will build strong connections. This improves your SEO too, because if the other person were to link to your blog from their own website, it gives you a higher ranking online.

On a weekly basis, make sure you are reaching out to at least one new person in your field, either via a personal email, through Facebook or in a blog that includes them. Once you have written your blog, it's important to share it far and wide (and often). Place the link to it in the groups you are permitted to share content in, use it to give value in comments when someone has an issue it could help with. Send it to your email list. In short, get it into as many places as you can. Now that you have a list of the most popular blogs in your field, it's worth connecting with the owners to see if you could guest blog on their site. Bloggers are always looking to include engaging, relevant content, so if you can provide something of value to their audience, reach out to them. Other great places to guest blog are places such as *Thrive Global*, *Huffington Post* and *Forbes*. Remember, you are a business, and what you do may be of interest to other businesses. You'll often find in *Entrepreneur & Business Facebook Groups* requests for Guest Bloggers. Take up some of these opportunities as they arise or actively request opportunities. Remember, although you are sharing your thoughts in your voice, your blog is not about you. It is about the reader, particularly the one who is your ideal client. Why would someone want to read what you have to say? What do they need to know? These are the basis of the topics you can write about to share your expertise.Now that you've identified the industry leaders, it's time to have a look around and establish who your peers are. You could think of them as the 'competition' although personally I like to see everyone as a potential collaborator. For me, it's a case of *why see threat everywhere*? Your competitors won't have an identical audience to you, they won't have the unique experiences you've had, and the more value you can give to each other's audiences the better for both of you.

Who else has a group that might have a similar audience to the one you are starting to build? Who do you know that is doing something similar to you that hangs out in the same places: Online? In-person?

Collaboration gives each of you an opportunity to get in front of a wider audience that you wouldn't reach ordinarily. Done properly, collaborations can be effective for positioning, kudos and follower building.

What could you offer to someone else's audience?

Think about your special subjects, areas of expertise, free sample content, webinars, video training, downloads, *Facebook Live* interviews as a special guest, membership content. What could you offer to entice other collaborators to work with you? Guest blogging? *Facebook Lives* in your group? A chance to promote their free content to your audience?

This would mean you not only position yourself as connected and influential, but your audience or Facebook Group gets extra value through following you, which increases the feeling of reciprocity, a major key to inducing influence. You've brought them a valuable piece of content - they'll be much more willing to invest in working with you.

Live video

As I write this, video marketing is taking off and I don't mean the polished, professional style videos. By now I'm sure you'll have realised the power of video and in particular *Facebook Lives* and *IGTV* videos (on Instagram) for establishing authority. There is nothing quite like knowing many people will hear you talk about what you do and what you know as a driver for honing your expertise and passion! The fact that you are going to show up and do it regularly raises you above the crowd. Being consistently visible, sharing your knowledge and experience - I promise - will pay dividends. The sooner you start doing live video, the sooner you'll improve at it. There are some simple steps to make your *Facebook Lives* more effective.

Most people watch video on their phones with the sound off, so you must grab attention in the first two seconds with NO SOUND, by using your hands or making some movement to grab their attention. Captions are good to use, too. You can add these in the settings on Facebook after you've completed your live video. Or you can use a service such as *Rev* where they send you the annotated captions in an hour or two, ready for you to upload alongside your video. Always make sure your check the captions are grammatically correct and follow the speed of your speech though, as these imperfections and delays can be irritating for viewers.

Before you start your *Facebook Live* video, know what result you want from it. Are you looking to get engagement? Do you want to establish authority? Do you have a freebie you want them to download? Or a Discovery Call you'd like them to book? Start with the end in mind so that the Call to Action seems integral.

Before you go live, write an interesting title for your video. The title of your *Facebook Live* can make a big difference as to whether someone will stop scrolling past your video as most people are watching with the sound switched off. Make your title stand out as a compelling headline so that if they come across your video on replay they are more likely to be intrigued and stop to watch. Good title ideas are 'How to… in 3 simple steps' or 'The 5 biggest mistakes …'. I highly recommend learning about effective headlines by doing a Google search into top headlines by leading marketers. This knowledge is transferrable to your email marketing headlines also. Write something that creates curiosity or that offers simplistic solution for overcoming a client's pain point, and you'll get much greater response and engagement.

Facebook Lives work best when you already have an idea of the content you want to share but are unscripted and in flow. When you start out, make sure you introduce yourself and what you do. Go back to your pitch work and include this as well as a request to 'like', 'type #replay', or ask them to 'share'. Keep your introduction simple, short and snappy and move on to the content you want to share with them.

Pre-Frame the information you are going to share, so they know what is coming up next and are more likely to keep watching. For example, 'In this Live I'll be sharing the top ways to ….' Give lots of value in your content. Your aim is always to show that you know your stuff, are passionate about your topic and confident talking about the results you get. This will position you as an authority with expertise. Even sharing your musings, learnings, obstacles and vulnerabilities can have this effect. Don't worry about giving too much of value away - this is how you build trust. Before someone chooses to work with you, they have to buy-in to you. Showing up on video gives them ample opportunity to see the real you.

The best way to do *Lives* is to go unscripted but prepare the shape of the content beforehand. Use post-it notes to keep yourself on track, including the Call to Action at the end. Get your audience accustomed to following your instructions early on so that when you come to sell your services, they are more likely to take action. Make sure you interact with viewers and welcome people who join you by name to make them feel valued. Most people will watch on replay, so even if someone comes in and then leaves, it's not personal! When you come to the end of the live broadcast, finish with a CTA (Call to Action). Be direct and clear on what action they should take next. This is a powerful, free way to build your authority and reach a wider audience.

I know that any form of live video has many people wanting to run a mile. I promise you that they are worth investing your time in. You're probably concerned that you'll go wrong or fluff up what you want to say. Don't worry. No one is perfect when they start out with live video. I was terrible a couple of years ago, really stilted and measured in what I said. Now though, it is part of a daily routine for me. I show up, I give value, I'm myself. I don't fret over being too polished, and on many occasions it is when I am less prepared that the videos achieve more comments and engagement. What I've found also is that most people will not comment, but they are there, watching. Many months later, a potential client will reach out to enquire about working together, and they will recall a specific moment about myself in a specific live that I shared about. Every single piece of video or audio content that I put out into the ether adds up to the results I now achieve. Allow yourself to be imperfect. Allow yourself to fail. You will improve with every live video you do, until it becomes second nature. There is no quicker way to build your business than live video right now.

Eradicating Imposter Syndrome

In this chapter I've shared lots of ideas on how to increase your authority. Before we close, though, I want to touch briefly on the concept of *Imposter Syndrome*. This is the feeling or belief that you will be caught out as being a fraud or not good enough at what you do. It is a common issue among people, especially high achievers. *Imposter Syndrome* can stop you from doing any of the activities I've mentioned in this chapter - from posting on social media, sending emails to your mailing list, contacting people of influence. It is perfectly normal to think this way, however it is not NECESSARY to let this fear get the better of you. If you notice these fears cropping up, go back and visit the *Inner Critic* section in this book and evaluate your limiting thoughts. They are only a story, not the truth of who you are. You have every right to be an authority, to increase your influence and to share your knowledge, expertise and learnings. You have every right to get visible.

8

VISIBLE SUCCESS AND BRINGING IN THE MONEY

The decision to get more visible can have many drivers: to lead a bigger life, to effect more change, to bring a significant financial figure into the bank. Part of this is showing and telling the world that you are good at what you do. This can be tricky when you are at the start of a new venture. How can you show that you are successful when you do not yet have the financial rewards or industry recognition to prove it? There are so many ways in which clients of mine have sabotaged their income possibilities by hiding their talents and abilities, or by not believing they deserve money (prior to working with me on their visibility mindset, of course).

Their beliefs around their ability to be trusted with money keep them frustrated with the financial results they get. In this chapter we'll be exploring your thoughts around money blocks and your personal limitations, and

I'll share with you my own story about money beliefs connected with fear, threat and danger and how I overcame them to charge more, earn more and set my own rates.

When you increase your worth in other people's eyes, you open doors to commanding and receiving higher fees. In order to do this, though, you first have to believe you deserve to charge a suitable amount. Second, you have to recognise and overcome past behaviours and patterns around money. Third, you need to learn the skills for getting someone who knows about you and what you do to become a paying, loyal customer or client.

When I initially decided to create a personal development online business, my lack of knowledge around converting an audience into potential leads was frustrating. It was damaging for my self-esteem and my business. After all, how can I be telling people that you can create anything that you want in your life if I'm struggling with bringing in enough clients to support the income and lifestyle I desire? The truth was that in my eagerness and determination to get out and help as many people with changing their lives, I had not known that that some vital pieces of the business puzzle were missing. I'm now grateful for the hurdles I fell at, since my learnings give me more to share with you about the financial part of the success jigsaw.

No matter what service or business you run, the bottom line is that you need it to bring in money. You can't impact lives if you're struggling financially. You can't reach all the people you want to help. The truth is, if you aren't bringing in enough to pay the bills, you aren't yet running a business. Once you learn the fundamentals of attracting the right people on social media and getting people in your networking circles to show interest in your work, you can begin the process of warming them up to become paying clients.

I'll be honest with you. This is the chapter that has had me stalling for weeks because to give this chapter all I've got, I had to share my own money story. Talking about money makes us uncomfortable, as if there is something unpleasant in setting our fees and stating our worth.

My money story

For years I would yo-yo with money. If I'd booked a new job or a new client, or if it was payday when I was employed, I would effectively spend the money before it arrived in my bank account. I would often hold myself back from going after high-paying jobs and scrabble around for the low fees. This did not feel good at all. It was only when closely examining my relationship with money that some beliefs around money came to light. When I was a child we lived in an area where we had lots of friends. We could play out in the street and cycle where we liked. We had good neighbours and it felt safe. When I was five years old, we were all set to move to a brand new estate - a real step up for us. My dad earned a significant amount of money for one job and it meant that we could now live in a much bigger 'posh' house. As a child, much is kept from you - you only hear half a story. The day the removal van arrived and parked outside our home, mum cried. It didn't make sense to me - we were supposed to be excited. My next memory of that time, perhaps a few days later, was of being in our new house in my nightdress, freshly bathed with wet hair looking down our long, shared driveway. There were armed policemen carrying guns walking to and fro in front of our house and all around the estate. I was told to come away from the window and not look at them.

This image played in my dreams for many months, if not years. It was frightening to have moved from some-where I felt safe and supported to a house that was clearly far from safe.

There were many whispered conversations around us children at that time. We knew that our brand new neigh-bour had been shot in bed in the middle of the night and that instead of shooting him in the heart, his finger had been blown off. They were a family of five, like us. The three children were asleep in their beds, and the news on TV said that the bad man had entered their bedrooms, that the bad man had stayed in our garage overnight during the week before we moved in and just before he attacked the other family.

As an adult, I learned that there had been a notorious

attacker on the run in Bedfordshire and Buckinghamshire known as 'The Fox', who terrorised the local area, doing unspeakable things. As a child, I pieced together small fragments and picked up on the massive amounts of fear surrounding these episodes.

Somewhere, deep in my unconscious, a story that it was not safe to have large amounts of money began to unfold. In my brain's efforts to protect me as an adult, whenever I earned money, I was driven to spend it. This played havoc with my finances. Acknowledging this limiting decision around earning, having and keeping money has changed my income dramatically as well as the decision to charge more for my work.

Years later I met a business coach on a flight back from New York and we connected instantly. Meeting Gael was one of those serendipitous moments I shall never forget. We needed each other's help and met at exactly the right moment for us both. She questioned me on my voiceover rates and the income I was producing. Was I charging enough? Could I get a bigger return for the same amount of work if I changed my beliefs about what I was capable and deserving of earning? This raised some interesting thoughts. At the time, I was focusing on building a portfolio of radio commercial work, based in the UK. These commercials could earn me anything from £18 to £100 depending on the radio station. The amount of work it required, once I had all of the necessary skills and recording abilities, was less than 30 minutes for about 30 seconds of finished audio. Gael challenged me to think bigger. Instead of focusing on the UK market, what would happen if I went after the top US national radio commercials? With so many listeners across the States, a single 30 second commercial could net me in excess of $30,000, with repeat fees on top. Why would I waste my time scrabbling around for low fees when there were big fees to be had for the same level of work? I was full of excuses - *I'm not experienced enough yet, I don't have the contacts yet, I don't have the authority or credibility yet.* Gael showed me that it would take the same amount of work that I was doing, but for a much greater reward. Whilst many people will go after the low figures, few have the gumption to go after the high ticket bookings. The work is the same whilst the confidence levels and deliberate positioning of credibility and authority are streets away. As you can imagine, it entirely altered my focus of attention, and that conversion is one of the reasons I later found myself in Hollywood. I decided to stop scrabbling for pennies and go for gold.

Your money mindset

Let's look at your *money mindset* - the beliefs that have kept you fearful around the topic of money. It doesn't have to be as dramatic as a gunman terrorizing your neighbourhood, however, the discussions you heard or the feelings you had around money during childhood can shape the story you unconsciously tell yourself about it, and no matter how hard you strive to change your money habits, something prevents you from charging more.

"Money makes the world go round."

We feel the impact of money every day in almost everything we do. It is such a fundamental part of modern life and yet ushers in so many unexplored fears - *that we'll never have any, that there isn't enough for us, that we don't deserve it.* Or conversely, that if we *were* to have it, we would be disliked, unpopular, unkind. If you've completed the work in earlier chapters, it'll come as no surprise that you can shift all of these thoughts and open yourself up to new possibilities concerning money.

We'll examine what your current thoughts about money are, where they came from and how often you vocalise or act on these beliefs. And then comes the exciting part. Through this chapter, combined with a free, powerful online visualisation audio (download at www.annaparkernaples.co.uk/money-making-audio) we're going to shift your blockages around money in subtle yet significant ways. It's game-changing work, so let's not hang about!

Complete the following statements as fully as you can. Be aware of all the thoughts, feelings and memories that flit through your mind. Sometimes the smallest moments in our recollection can give huge clues as to our perceptions of money and our own worthiness.

Activity: My childhood & money

Complete the following:

The comments I heard about money were:

I knew this meant that having money was:

My Mum thought money was:

My Dad thought money would:

For their relationship, it meant that:

For our family, the amount of money we had meant that we could have:

And that we couldn't have:

This made me feel:

Activity: Old money beliefs

Now we're going to investigate some of the beliefs you hold about money. Fill in the following phrases without stopping to think about them too much. It's your first response that is often quite telling.

Rich people are:

Not everyone can be wealthy because:

I'm not meant to have the money I want because:

The reason I've not got enough money is:

The people or person I blame for not having all that I want financially is:

'Money is the source of all evil' is a comment I have heard, and I see this when:

The main reason I don't have money is:

When it comes to saving and investing, I usually:

To me, budgeting and planning is:

Activity: What I say about money

So far, we've begun to unravel some of the beliefs that hold you back from having the abundance you desire in your life. Over the next few days, I would like you to notice any time you mention money, cost or being able to afford something. Often, the way we speak about money, particularly with our children, can be revealing. See if you can identify when and how often you are repeating any phrases such as:

Money doesn't grow on trees.

I'm not made of money.

Don't be wasteful.

I haven't got any money

I don't have enough

We can't afford it

We're saving for a rainy day/in case of emergencies

The taxman takes all our money.

You have to work hard to make any money.

Not everyone is loaded.

Write down all examples of frequent sayings you use about money. Take a note of how you felt when you said it and the impact this has on you. Add to this list as you go through your week. The more limiting thoughts and sayings about money you can catch yourself giving attention to, the greater your ability to make some shifts.

My old familiar money sayings:

Activity: What if I had money?

What would happen in your life if you believed money could come to you easily whenever you put your mind to it? What difference would that make to the work you do? If that question caused any resistance or tension in you, jot down your limiting thoughts here:

Now that you've acknowledged those darker thoughts around money, put the limitations aside and allow yourself to dream during this next exercise. Let's imagine that money can and does come to your frequently and easily.

What kind of life would that enable you to lead?

Now that money is no object I can:

The people I'm able to help are:

The impact I have on the world now that I have money is:

Once I have all the money I need to live my highest purpose and follow my dreams, I would bring the following to my relationships:

The difference this would make to my life is:

Activity: A force for good

Write out as many ways you can think of that money has a positive impact on the world:

List five wealthy people who use their money to do good things:

Write out your own dream life with money. What would a typical day look like and how would you feel?

What would you be doing and who would be with you?

Be as specific and detailed as you can (add to it in your journal if you have a lot more to say. Dream big!)

Activity: New money thoughts

Let's start to create a bank of positive statements around money. These can be useful for reframing some of the negative language you identified earlier, and through repetition transform your neural pathways. The more you say and think them, the easier it will be to access those thoughts and the greater the influence this new thought will have on your mind and your reality:

I am grateful to money because:

I can attract money into my life by:

Money has helped me to:

I have all the money I need at my disposal which gives me the confidence to:

I have the ability to make money by:

Noticing my old money habits and now thinking more beneficial thoughts about money gives me the power to:

Activity: Money Abundance - take control of your finances

If you don't know how much money you currently have, how can you be grateful for it? If you don't have an understanding of your present debt situation, how can you celebrate when your wealth improves?

Diarise a few hours to go through your finances and get a handle on where your money goes. Look at all the things you already afford. (Don't focus on the past struggle to pay for those things, focus on your gratitude for making it happen).

In all areas of self-development, taking responsibility for your thoughts, actions and behaviours puts you in a position of power. Money and finances are no exception. No matter how scary or off-putting it seems, taking time to get wise to your financial situation as it stands puts you in the driving seat and allows you to take control.

Activity: Money mantras

Write out daily the following money mantras and repeat them to yourself when you catch yourself uttering an old limiting belief about money:

Money flows to me easily and effortlessly.

I am just as deserving of having all the money I desire as anybody else.

Anyone can attract, make and keep money if they commit to it, and so can I.

I love money because it allows me to express more and more of who I am.

I am prepared to take action to make the money that I desire, because I am just as capable and competent as anybody else.

I am taking charge of growing my finances and this empowers me.

Money is a good force in my life and I'm ready and open for more of it.

If you notice any resistance to these statements, write out your negative belief and see if you can turn it around to a new, more empowering sentence. Visit these mantras as often as you can through the coming months and notice any improvements in your money outlook. Combine this work with using the free *Money Making Mindset* visualisation track (www.annaparkernaples.co.uk/money-making-audio). As you *become* more visible, this work around money beliefs will enable you to reap the rewards of creating more visibility.

9

STANDOUT SUCCESS

Let's face it, getting visible is about standing out from the crowd. This chapter will explore ways to increase your profile and upscale your visibility. We'll be looking at the benefits of becoming a speaker, attending events, running online and offline events and the power of award nominations. We'll look at the importance of getting Press and PR interest, not only from a business strategy point of view, but from a personal angle to help you overcome those fears about being seen on national and international platforms. We'll explore other media platforms and how you can 'own your space' in a way that has never previously been so accessible. Podcasts and webinars are booming right now and we'll have a look at how these can be used to scale influence and reach larger audiences - to stand out from the crowd. I'll share my experience of running audio *and* visual content on both of these online platforms and show the differences they can make to your kudos, credibility and bank balance.

Back to basics. I've talked about knowing who you help and why. What I've not covered in detail is how you can make sure you elevate yourself from others, who essentially do the same work as you. My biggest piece of advice is to drill down on your niche. You want to be THE expert in a given area, not *someone* who can help *anyone*. You want to be the one who comes to mind for a deliberate and intentional element of what you do. For example, in my voice work, as I mentioned before, I wasn't just a female voiceover. I crafted myself as the native British female audiobook narrator specialising in Young Adult Fiction voice work. Niche, upon niche, upon niche. As a Business and Mindset Coach, I'm not just a coach. I help ambitious, purpose-driven entrepreneurs who want to impact lives and therefore the world by increasing their visibility and getting their message out to more people. I'm a Visibility Expert and Podcast Coach. As a Motivational Speaker, I don't just motivate people. I speak on how to overcome fears around becoming visible and successful or on ways to use podcasting to build authority. I urge you to look at what everyone else is doing in your industry and think to yourself, what can I do differently?

The sooner you get specific, the quicker people will know who to refer to you. You become memorable, no longer vanilla and generic but a flavour that resonates with the right kind of people. Think exotic mango sorbet with tutti fruity topping. Anyone can be vanilla …

Look at ways you can stand out from the crowd when you network or appear online. Part of my current branding has a flavour of red with a hint of a vintage British feel, so I incorporate an element of this into how I present myself. A touch of red here and there, a branding photo shoot that encapsulates that feel. Previously in voice work, I used a vivid, energetic green colour and every-thing I put out into the world had a hint of green - my outfits, the background of my photos. The tiniest detail can make a difference and help you stick in someone's mind. For example, if you were a man regularly attending networking events and everyone else is in a suit, shirt and tie, you would be memorable if you wore a colourful striped shirt. There is a line, of course - you don't want to be a caricature of yourself. But in a busy, crowded industry it is worth giving thought to the simplest details.

Create yourself as someone who is seen and heard at all the significant events. When you walk into that room, be noticed and be able to communicate your area of expertise.

Hosting your own event

Organise your own events. With the right people in the room, high quality photography to capture the day and a clever launch and post-launch strategy, hosting your own event can catapult your presence and gravitas in the eyes of your audience.

Tips for hosting your event

Start small. It is better to begin with an event that is likely to sell out and drive people to a waiting list (thereby creating a sense of demand and urgency for your next event) than to create one that will be less than half full of attendees. In the early stages of running events, the value is in the buzz you create. Make your event limited in numbers, make it exclusive, and go all in with inducing FOMO (fear of missing out) for those that can't make it. The event you run will be an extension of you and your personal brand. How you make people feel and the experience they have with you in the room matters.

The best investment you can make is to employ the services of a professional photographer. High quality images are part of your long-term positioning strategy and create desire in the rest of your audience who did not attend, thereby driving a need to attend your next one. You can use events to launch a new product or service so that they become a vital part of your sales strategy rather than a one-off occasion. I recently hosted an event to coincide with my Entrepreneurs Get Visible podcast launch. This enabled me to influence the number of downloads and reviews given on iTunes at a specific time.

After the event, make sure you get testimonials and feedback as these are invaluable resources for future events and promotions. If you can get video testimonials, even better. They are powerful stuff.

There are many event organisers who provide venue searches for free. They make their money through the commission they receive from a venue if you decide to book. They will have good knowledge of suitable locations for your budget and they'll be well-placed to help you if you need assistance with creating a quality experience.

There is something powerful about being in a room with people. Your attendees are likely to be your ideal clients and the rapport, relationship and trust you build through giving them value and sharing your expertise can make them feel much more attached and loyal to you. Since I introduced casual, occasional meet-ups into my paid membership for entrepreneurs, those bonds and attachments have increased, making it much easier to convince people to take action to work with me on my courses and one-to-one coaching. They have already bought in to me and what I do to some degree. And the relationships they foster with each other provides an increased desire to keep learning alongside one another.

What kind of event could you consider? (Casual meet up workshop/conference-style/ networking/party)
What budget could you put towards the event?
How many people would you ideally have in attendance?
What value/learning would they receive on the day?

Who will be involved? Just you, or guests and speakers?
Will you need an assistant?
What Early Bird and Full Price tickets could you offer?
How much profit would you need to make to ensure the event is worthwhile financially?

Award events

My absolute favourite way to boost my visibility is to attend awards events. And, of course, to apply for awards if appropriate and to be nominated by someone else. Naturally, the best way to leverage publicity is to win, but this not the only way in which awards are useful to your visibility.

Attending a relevant high-profile awards event was the biggest game-changer for me early on in my voice career, and I replicated it when my professional focus changed. Applying for suitable awards will remain high on my list of business activities.

Earlier I described how, once I had decided to 'go big or go home' in the audiobook industry my success transformed. This level of niching is possible whatever field you are in. I flew to that event in New York knowing that the majority of the significant industry leaders and decision-makers would be there. I knew nobody in that room but being intentional about who I wanted to meet and what I could bring to the table changed everything. The commitment and belief I displayed by attending that event solo showed that I was a serious contender in the industry. I stood out.

Within a year I was nominated, a finalist and winning my first international awards. It is no coincidence. I had chosen and sought out opportunities to connect and network at the events that counted. I was seen and heard in places of influence. That's powerful. It made me memorable; it allowed me access to people I could never have initiated conversations with online. Personal connection and rapport matters. In most instances, anyone can purchase a ticket to an awards gala. It is worth attending an event if you know who is likely to be in the room, for a simple opportunity to make casual acquaintance, oftentimes at the bar as you order a drink.

Activity: Awards

List all award events, both industry and business-related, that are relevant to your field, or that celebrate small businesses. These can be local, national and international.

Most award events are annual occasions, so you can work out when they are most likely to happen. The networking element of a gala tends to happen before the awards are announced, so it is a good idea to arrive early and be ready to work the room.

There is a lot of mileage in being able to tell

people that you have won an award for your work. Not only does it give you credibility, it also provides plenty of scope for getting in local and national press.

And - becoming an awards finalist can generate as many opportunities as winning. If you attend the event itself then you can gain valuable social proof photos. In most instances you would have usually been provided with an award finalist logo that you can share in your marketing.

The protocol of nominating yourself

A lot of entrepreneurs I work with worry that it is egotistical or false to nominate yourself for an award. I challenge that. The whole awards industry is designed to elevate status and bring recognition. Many of the major awards like the Oscars contain some element of self-nomination in the early stages. Awards are an effective game and if you aren't courageous enough to play, you can bet one of your competitors will. It is commonplace for people to nominate themselves – it's just that nobody talks about it. The only thing stopping you from getting that badge of recognition is your own fear that you don't deserve it, or that because you have put yourself in the ring it isn't a valid award to win. That's your limiting beliefs and inner critic raising their voices. As long as there is a panel of judges and a fair, open judging policy, there is no reason not to put yourself up for nomination.

Locally, there are often awards categories that actively promote the *rising star* or the *new business*, and if you are just starting out with incorporating award nominations into your visibility strategy, start here.

Activity: Local awards

Do a full Google search into suitable award events and write down categories that might be applicable to you and your business.

Usually, there is a fee to place a nomination. However, when you consider the increased publicity, it is absolutely a good investment. Think of applying for awards as a valuable, yet relatively inexpensive marketing tool, and play the game to your advantage. You can garner exposure, press and PR as a result of just being a nominee, never mind becoming a finalist. In many respects, the award itself doesn't matter. It is how others perceive its value that matters.

The awards I was finalist for in Hollywood, I didn't win. But that is irrelevant. The prestige, the build-up, the anticipation - those things made a difference to how the rest of my industry saw me, and to how my friends, acquaintances and peers viewed what I did. It didn't take long before I was receiving referrals for all sorts of work from all sorts of avenues as a result of posting the first pictures of me as an award nominee. When I switched my professional focus and entered the world of mindset and sharing my personal story, the award I won amongst celebrities such as Rio Ferdinand, Holly Willoughby and Adele gave me enormous amounts of validity. And those associations don't vanish, they become a part of the fabric of my credibility and online persona, a part of my online footprint no matter which direction I go in. So - give it a go. Apply for something to celebrate your business and put the work you do on the map. The week I was announced as a finalist for *Business Woman of the Year* and *Entrepreneur of the Year*, I was inundated with enquiries about working with me one-to-one, not to mention the impact winning in those categories had several months later.

Activity: Relevant national and international awards

Make a list of **all** awards and relevant categories you could apply for. Note the application opening/closing dates and events dates. Get them in your diary, and make sure you are in that room.

Get yourself in the Press

I cannot write a book on visibility within talking about getting yourself in the Press. Media exposure can transform your business. It allows you to get your message out to people you just cannot reach through your own marketing efforts.

One of the best ways to get PR is to work closely with a Public Relations agency. There tends to be two models - *proactive* and *reactive* PR. For proactive PR the agency will create a campaign around you. This is useful once you have a higher profile, or when you have a book or similar ready for release. It's more expensive as it involves targeted, focused work from the PR team.

Reactive PR is perhaps easier to generate. Journalists and media professionals are often on the look-out for featured quotes. Usually they have already written the piece, or have a strong outline for it, and are looking for people to place comment. This could be a piece about your area of expertise and a chance to be featured in a non-related topic that shares a part of your personal story. For example, I have featured in newspapers and magazines as a result of my difficult pregnancy story and in relation to overcoming depression.

As I write this chapter, I've just had notification that I've been featured in the national publication *Metro*, both online and in print, with an article about the *Couch to 5k* programme and how being spurred on by Tony Robbins' audiobook *Awaken the Giant Within* made me take the final steps in my recovery to start running again. Last week I was featured in an international article on *Yahoo News* about how working from home can affect your mental health and how we decided to get a dog to make sure I get out into the fresh air every day. Neither topics are my speciality, but I can talk on both. I have curated images of parts of my life that make me appealing for journalists and editors, and I have, together with my PR team, done the groundwork to prepare my story so that I can provide valid, valuable comment. I am not fearful of getting out there. I am no longer afraid to be seen, to be heard and to be remembered. I know that it is all a part of increasing and maintaining visibility.

Often, a journalist will allow a reference to the line of work I am now in or even share details of my website or social media handles. This enables me to reach a wider audience than I could ever have found on my own. Like-wise, a friend who specialises in divorce coaching recently appeared in a women's magazine with a *before and after* photo of how she was taking part in a dance competition. The makeover wasn't focused on what she does now, but there was mention of the journey she had been on. Great exposure. Another entrepreneurial friend of mine specialising in financial education for women took part in a mental health awareness campaign because of her struggle with an eating disorder. She positioned her expertise around the personal, vulnerable story she shares. Think out of the box about what stories you could share, because both expertise and personal story articles are useful for gaining press.

What areas of your work could you provide comment on?

What interesting parts of your story could be useful to a journalist (think Women's Magazines - the *real life* sections often allow a link to your website).

If you are not yet in a position to work with a PR team, there are some ways to gain exposure yourself. Why not email the publications' editors directly?

Tips for emailing editors:

Keep your email succinct and to the point.

Do not expect a reply!

Follow your query up a few weeks later to remind them that you are a valuable source. This is especially true if a newsworthy event takes place that you could add comment or opinion on.

Stay abreast of hot topics on social media and the news. If a subject is trending, you can bet your bottom dollar there are several journalists looking for sources to interview or quote, so the more aware you are, the better your chance of landing in the right inbox at the right time.

Although I often work with a PR team, I have secured some excellent features myself. When I began working in the mindset and success space, I chose publications that I would like to appear in and contacted the editors directly. As a result, my new business venture appeared in *Psychologies* magazine (the UK's leading personal development print magazine), *Happiful, Kindred Spirit* and *Health and Wellbeing* within weeks of launching a brand new business.

Do be aware though that journalists may not quote you directly and may alter what you have said to fit their own ideas. Still, all exposure is good exposure if it helps you to get seen and heard. The same applies to radio interviews. You are led very much by the agenda of the interviewer, who may not be terribly receptive to what you and your business represent. I learnt this the hard way on air, when a male interviewer, the 'star' of the radio station, decided that a mum-focused business was inherently sexist. It was challenging, but I kept a level head (and my cool), and had several people reach out to tell me how professionally I came across despite his misguided line of questioning.

Activity: Which publications do you want to be seen in?

_____

Make a list of publications you would like to appear in and do a search on the name of the editor:

Activity: Which radio stations do you want to be heard on?

Local radio shows are always on the look-out for interesting guests. Research your local stations and find out which producers are interested in people for interviews:

Activity: Tweet

A great way to get in touch with journalists is through Twitter. Regular posts with #journorequest or #PRrequest are placed with a brief synopsis of what they are looking for. Spend a few minutes a day having a look over the requests. Quite often the turnarounds and deadlines will be tight and journalists will expect you to be prepared with a media bio and quotes ready to go.

Conduct a search over the past month to see the kind of posts that might have been suitable for you.

What kind of quotes are journalists looking for?

What timeline is there for responding?

Is anything else required to respond, such as a photo or a bio?

Brand associations

People are often persuaded to purchase from you as a result of personal recommendation or social proof and 'authority tags' such as places you have been featured or mentioned or connections in your network. The more social proof you can gather and share, the better your results will be. Two ways to give social proof of your work are brand logos and testimonials.

Being able to show that you have been featured *in*, or *by* a particular media outlet is valuable currency. It is one way to elevate you amongst your industry peers and it's one of the reasons PR makes such a difference to your business results. Find ways to promote who you have worked with or been featured by. You can include the logos on your Facebook Page, your Facebook Profile and LinkedIn banners and your websites (as long as you have written permission to do so).

Which brands and associations can you include (or deliberately pursue) that will add to your prestige?

Testimonials

Personal testimonials are crucial. On landing/sales pages and your main website, a testimonial with a photo of the individual, full name and company has even more impact. Make it your number one aim to receive a testimonial for every piece of work you do. Break longer testimonials down into smaller parts. These can be interspersed amongst your social media. You cannot post your professional successes and feedback too much!

Asking for written, online referrals as part of your everyday business activity makes a difference. Streamline the process and you'll end up with ample public recommendations. One useful trick on LinkedIn is to spend time giving referrals to others in your networks whilst asking for nothing in return. The human need for reciprocity will instill a desire to return the favour. It's worth trying and testing.

Who can you reach out to now for a testimonial?

Professional bio

When approaching journalists and editors, or even potential collaborators, it is essential to have your professional bio and business life story shaped and ready to share. A professional biography shows your skills, expertise and background. It can be used on your social media profiles, in formal introductions and when you are pitching for collaborations. Revisit the *pitch* section earlier in this book before you write your bio.

Here are my top tips for writing your professional biography:

Write in the third person so that it sounds objective and professional.

Begin with a sentence that includes your name and what your business is. Then, mention the accomplishments that are most relevant to your field of work.

Include something that your audience/ideal client would relate to.

End with a sentence on projects you are or have been working on.

Try to keep your bio to around 100-300 words depending on where you need to put it. (It's useful to have two versions ready to go - one long and one short).

Your bio is your introduction to your audience and potential clients. It should communicate who you are and what you do. It should state your claim to fame. What are you known for? What makes you the go-to person? What makes you an expert? What experience/ expertise do you have? What are your accomplishments? Describe them. Awards? List them.

Activity: My accomplishments

Describe your accomplishments:

If you recall the work we did in Chapter 5, Crafting your Credibility, you'll remember that there is much that you have accomplished which has become second nature to you. You are the perfect person to do what you are now doing. Leave nothing unsaid - the smallest thing will inspire your audience.

Include personal, relatable and humanising details. This is a nice way to build rapport with the reader. It's also your chance to get some of your personality across. Ideally, these personal details will attract your audience to YOU and serve as conversation-starters should you meet them in real life.

To complete your bio, include details of projects you have coming up, for example, a qualification you're working towards, a book you are writing, media you're due to publish in, an event you're speaking at or a place you're volunteering with. This should be kept to a sentence or two.

As you develop and grow, ensure you keep your bio up-to-date and refresh as necessary. As your business expands and evolves, you'll be amazed at how much your bio does too!

Activity: Write out your full new bio:

Speaker Opportunities

Becoming a speaker in your industry or local networking community can pay huge dividends for your authority and credibility (and ultimately your profit). Not everyone has the skills or ability to stand on stage and command an audience, so if this is in your toolkit, or you want it to be, get your business head on and work out the places you can be seen on stage. An important thing to remember, though, is that no matter what your subject is, if it contains elements of your personal story, you MUST keep it relevant to the audience and their needs. Your talk is about them, not about you. When I first started out as a speaker, I knew I had an epic tale to tell. Not everyone can share a journey from disabled and depressed to the red carpets of Hollywood and multi-award-winning coach. However, it is not my story that matters. What matters are the takeaways I give to my audience about how to raise their visibility. My story might inspire and motivate them and perhaps make them realise how much they have been hiding or self-sabotaging their results, but the specific actions that they can implement from my talk makes the difference. I need to be able to convey why my talk is relevant to them and their life and the benefits of taking notice of what I teach. Again, my talk isn't about me. It's about what it enables others to unlock.

Think about the value you can bring to people with your knowledge and skills. What can you talk about?

Now think about who might be interested in your message.

What kind of places might they attend? (formal corporate workplaces/networking/events/conferences).

Start small. Can you give a short talk at a local event? Speakers are always required to fill these slots and it is a good way to become a local celebrity. Remember, you do not need to have years of experience to be an expert. Most of the people in the room do not have your level of understanding about your chosen field.

Where could you offer to speak locally?

Where could you offer to speak for your industry? Who do you need to contact?

Initially, you will find opportunities to speak for free. However, once you have some experience and credibility you'll be able to charge for your speaking engagements.

Top tips to build your speaker profile:

- Ensure you get good photographs (these are worth more than the speaking event itself!)
- Get high quality footage for your showreel, including not only close-ups of your talk but cut-aways that include the size of your audience and audience response to your talk.
- Get testimonials from attendees after your talk, preferably captured on video.
- Request a testimonial, preferably to video, from the event organiser.
- Create a demo of your footage and testimonials.
- Create a Speaker section on your website. It must be clear that this something you are competent in.
- Thank organisers and ask for suggestions for other event promoters to contact.
- Give a strong *Call to Action* at the end of your talk asking people for recommendations for other speaking opportunities.

Activity: What do I have to say?

_____

Make a list of topics you could speak on:

_____

I began my speaking career on panel discussions and went from there. My first big talk was in Hollywood in front of almost 1000 attendees. I knew my subject ... I knew what I wanted to communicate. Since then I have spoken in the US and the UK on numerous subjects. Coming from a performance background, I had presentation skills, but these are definitely things you can learn and develop.

In crafting my speeches, I follow two models and weave them together. First, I follow a structure that appeals to all styles of learning, sharing the four steps of 'Why?', 'What?', 'How?' and, 'What if?' - finally encouraging them to think about how they can take action *right now*.

The *Why* section is at the top of my talk – explaining why this topic is significant to me, my audience and to humanity as a whole. It sets the tone for why paying attention and engaging in what is to come matters. It often evokes an emotional response. The *What* segment goes into the key concepts of the topic and presents opportunities to think about the subject and its wider implications. The *How* section is often more detailed, offering explanations on actions that can be taken to make a specific change or effect, and the *What If* section paints the picture of possibility for change when the *How's* and *What's* are implemented, and is often effective in inducing the desire to take action *now*.

Second, in crafting my talks, I find weaving in stories

effective for connecting with an audience and use some of my training in hypnotic language sequences to make my talks as compelling as possible. People are hardwired to love stories and the brain strives to find an attachment that it can understand unconsciously. Remember that filing cabinet I talked about in the first chapters of this book? Well, it is *story* that helps sift out meaning from what you say. Here is the model I often follow:

I begin with a story that connects with the topic. This might be personal or a generic story that relates to the audience's current needs, wants and desires. I tell 70-80% of that story, then switch to another story on a similar theme and again share 70-80% of it. At this point I would reach the core *teach* of my subject with a sentence or two that has weight, meaning or significance for what I want people to take away. This is often a command or instruction – the body and meat of the talk. I allow it to sink in, take a pause and then return to story number two, which I complete, before completing story number one. By following these methods, I know that I'm not only hitting all learning styles - all the ways people feel, think and process - but I'm also tapping into a primal response to absorb stories. This structure enables change and understanding at both a conscious and unconscious level. There is so much more to teach on talk structure and delivery that would probably fill a whole other book, but I felt it too important to skip over.

Be a podcast guest

Sharing your story on as many platforms as possible is vital in order to reach as many people as possible, and I have found appearing on podcasts to be a foolproof way of building my audience by tapping into other people's. Podcasts are becoming the best free marketing tool on the planet. Podcast hosts are always looking for great guests, knowledgeable in their field, and through the intimate power of being a voice inside someone's car as they drive, or inside their head when they listen through earbuds, you can create powerful rapport with the listener who will in turn seek you out online to follow more of your musings. Another great thing about podcasts is that the host will promote your interview everywhere. Getting on the right podcasts for your industry can make a difference to your visibility and prestige. They are fantastic for stamping your authority. You get to be *you* - chatty and relaxed. And they provide long-term SEO.

When reaching out to a podcast host, there are a few simple guidelines:

1. Listen to the show first - preferably a couple of episodes - so that you understand its style.

2. Provide an image, brief bio and all of your social media handles upfront - it makes you a much more appealing guest.

3. Go back to your formal pitch and reshape a brief

version to suit the podcast's audience. What topics could you talk about that might be of relevance?

4. Keep the email short and to the point.

Activity: Appropriate podcasts

Make a list of podcasts in your area of expertise. Include both the well-known and the less well-known shows:

Who are the hosts?

What topics do they interview people on?

Which episode resonates with you? Why?

If you'd like to go into more detail to plan how to pitch to the right podcasts, download my free checklist at;

www.annaparkernaples.co.uk/income-from-interviews-checklist/.

It will give you all the information you need to ensure the interviews you give are useful not only in elevating your status, but from an income creating perspective too.

Hosting your own podcast

If you aren't already doing it, hosting your own podcast establishes your authority, niche and expertise in a way like no other. It gives you great SEO and a reason to reach out to those in your industry with bigger followings. It is also an easy way for your ideal client to find you. A podcast allows you to talk about the topics that matter to you and your ideal audience. It can be as chatty and relaxed or formal and structured as you like.

Anyone can host a podcast - you do not need permission. You can either create a show where you release new content on a weekly, fortnightly or monthly basis, or release a series of episodes around your topic.

With my 15 years background in audio, for me starting a podcast was a no-brainer. My *first podcast* grew with me as my business has changed, pivoted and evolved. And my second podcast Entrepreneurs Get Visible is an evolution of everything I learned about marketing, mindset and launching effectively. People often comment that they like my down-to-earth style as I talk through inspirational activities and my warts-and-all entrepreneurial journey. My podcast has grown steadily and many followers consume all of my previous podcast content once they've found me. I knew nothing about podcasts when I started. I just felt that they would be another way to attract clients. I now think of my podcast as the top of my funnel, and one of the most important business activities I can do. I give free, valuable content, I share knowledge, stories and experience. For many, that will be enough, and they will need nothing further from me to get started or continue their journey. For some, though, it is just the beginning. They find me through *iTunes, Stitcher* or *Spotify*. They like what I have to say, they relate to me. They sign up for my freebies, my lower level courses, my memberships. Overwhelming, though, is the number of listeners who have never interacted with me online, never reviewed, commented or shared my podcast … but who will contact me directly to work on my 3-month courses or my masterminds. You see, they have had me in their ears for hours, weeks, months. They have had me with them as they do chores, go for a run, travel the country. It's powerful, that intimate connection.

Podcasting

In theory, to get started in podcasting all you need is a simple USB microphone, a pop-shield to prevent 'popping' noises on certain words, somewhere relatively quiet to record in and basic editing software (such as *Audacity*) and some quality headphones. If you're concerned about editing, record straight into an online meeting service such as *Zoom* and then employ the services of a freelance audio editor (prices start from approximately £30 per hour of finished content). You can source these editors on platforms such as *Upwork* or *Freelancer*. For my up-to-date recommendations for equipment, visit

www.annaparkernaples.co.uk/podcastchecklist.

For me though, getting the concept for your podcast right from the offset makes a tremendous difference to its ratings, reviews and the subsequent influence your podcast can have. I'm interested in helping people launch with impact, not just have a podcast as yet another means to put content out there. Podcasting should be a pleasure, and an effective core of your business, when done well. Which is why you'll find far more detail about how to do it right in my book *Podcast with Impact.*

Podcasts can include interviews, your own musings, rants, raves and industry discussions. They can be as personal or formal in style as you like. Think about what suits you and your audience. How can you best convey what they want to hear, so that your show becomes a valuable resource?

A podcast is a great tool for directing people to your email list which ensures you have more ways later on to nurture them from *cold* to *hot* prospects and eventually sell to them. Each episode can drive listeners to your freebie, your group, your list - in fact you can signpost for listeners to take whatever action you like.

Creating podcast episodes does not have to be complicated. Some of your *Facebook Lives* can even be repurposed into a podcast episode with minor editing, likewise any Youtube content you have have created.

The platform I currently recommend for hosting my podcast is *Libsyn*. Through their service, my *Entrepreneurs Get Visible Podcast* episodes are automatically pushed to *iTunes, Spotify, Stitcher* and other significant and smaller podcast platforms. *Lisbyn* even creates a website specifically for your podcast if you choose to utilize it; alternatively it allows you to quickly create html code of your podcast audio so that you can embed the episode into your own website or blog.

When launching your podcast, follow a launch strategy as you would for any other service or offering by gaining interest, desire and hunger. Bringing in guests with bigger followings is a great way to increase your visibility, as they will often share your podcast with their own audience, getting more eyes (and ears) on you and your content. You can also earn through sponsorship, affiliations and providing additional content for your followers. It's worth investigating a platform called *Patreon* to find out more about building additional income streams into your podcast with paid premium content levels.

Activity: My podcast

_____

Jot down a few ideas on what you could include on your own podcast:

Since writing the first edition of Get Visible, I have established The Podcast Membership for those who want to learn how to podcast effectively for themselves, and I am CEO of my own Podcast Production Agency for those who want to concentrate on their important message and have the rest of their show taken care of. To find out about our fully 'done-for-you' service and launch consultancy, go to www.annaparkernaples.co.uk/podcast-production. We have helped many entrepreneurs, authors and experts launch impactful, chart-topping podcasts around the world. I have shared much of my podcast launch strategy inside my second book *Podcast with Impact: How to Start & Launch Your Podcast Properly.*

Webinars

Webinars are another great tool for establishing authority. A webinar is an online teaching with an interactive element. Hosting a webinar gives you an opportunity to showcase your knowledge and expertise, providing valuable learnings and creating potential sales. After all, followers have already received an in-depth training from you, understood that you know your field and been engaged in your teaching style for a significant amount of time. You have held their attention and given them useful, actionable steps to take in order to solve their pain points.

Some basic statistics for webinars:

50% of people who sign up for your webinar will actually attend.

20% of those who attend will sign up to your offer (provided you have given value).

40% of attendees will sign up on the actual day of the webinar, even if they have planned to attend from when they were first aware of it.

You can see, therefore, that getting people to attend your webinar is beneficial for whatever service or product you are providing. Like your email list, webinar sign-ups become a numbers game for driving revenue into your business.

You can run webinars with slides or directly to camera, either solo or with a guest/cohost. You can choose how much interaction you wish to have with your attendees and even decide the length of the session. You are fully in control and can dictate the pace. It is a brilliant way to stand out from the crowd.

To get sales from a webinar, the most important thing is to give value on the solutions your ideal client is seeking. Go back to the section on your ideal client's biggest struggles. Your webinar should address each of these.

If using a webinar for sales, begin with just you on camera in order to establish rapport with your attendees, then switch to screen-sharing and use of a presentation.

Make sure the first 75% of the training positions you, compellingly, as the expert and provides easy-to-implement solutions for your ideal clients' pain points. The latter 25% can switch to what you are offering to help them gain the benefits of your solution. Webinars can create a fantastic opportunity to share your knowledge, create community and drive sales through inducing scarcity.

Learning to launch

In the early days of my membership, before I understood launching, there was no 'need' to join. Most of my list and following *were* interested but they just didn't take the action to make the payment. Since they knew they could join at any time, there was no impulse to do it now, so the decision to purchase is delayed again and again, and then never happens. Once I learned the value and strategy of creating deliberate scarcity and limited time availability, I never looked back.

People decide to purchase either because a product or service will solve a problem or because it will create a result they desire. If there is an option to sign up to something without a time limit, there is no immediate pressure or demand to invest there and then, so most people will choose not to at that time. This is the case even if what you are offering is something they KNOW they want, and KNOW they intend to invest in. Unless you create scarcity and time-limits around your products and services, you will experience difficulty building your paying client and customer base.

In every part of your launch campaign you should consider how to create opportunities to sign up - to a wait list, freebie, group, webinar, bonus, Early Bird ticket, either in limited numbers available (e.g.*30 places available, first 10 to sign up receive....*) or limited in the amount of time they have to access the content (e.g. *available for 48 hours, wait list closing on...*) Those interested will take the action you instruct them to take. Since you have been instructing them to take your call to action in many posts and emails by now, they will be accustomed to taking the action you command. This is why sales are so popular in the high street, and why online events such as *Cyber Monday* generate increased revenue. It's all about inducing the need to take action immediately or face the consequences of missing out.

The Launch Process

Four to six weeks before your launch date, begin 'seeding' the idea for your service without revealing to your audience the details of what you are going to launch. Create a feeling of desire and need without giving the game away. Inducing curiosity, intrigue and FOMO (Fear of Missing Out) is paramount to getting the results you want.

Consider what you will do for your launch. Hold a

Facebook Live? Host a webinar and reveal your offer at the end? Run a 5 Day Challenge in your Facebook Group and unveil your offer on the final day? Remember, whilst you desire a result for your audience, the key thing about this pre-launch phase is positioning your expertise, building more trust and loyalty. The result should be to drive your audience to that specific event. All of your posts and emails should be focused on that result.

Always have a fixed date and time for your close cart and stick to it! In the long term this creates and encourages people to take action when you want them to. Once the cart closes, change your landing page to a *Wait List* for the next time you launch.

As a person of influence, one of the most valuable actions you can take is to thank your audience and followers on a regular basis. Email your list a day or two later to thank them for staying with you and to offer valuable content to help them. They'll have received a LOT of emails or posts from you in a short period. People will have unsubscribed from your list, and this is totally normal. They were never going to purchase from you, never going to be your ideal client. I'm always grateful to those who unsubscribe. I'm not right for them right now. It's not personal, so don't get wrapped up in the *rejection* story.

Every single sign-up to your offer is worth celebrating, whether or not you reach your targets. Each launch, you will get better and better and learn ways to improve. I know this seems like a lot of work the first time around, but trust me, once you understand and implement a launch strategy into your business you will thank me in the end! Launches give you tremendous opportunities to get your ideal clients aware of what you do with a concerted effort. A launch strategy will help them to get the result they want, to relieve the pain they are in. You are providing a service that they need, and that is valuable to them. You are just making that decision to purchase a little more compelling.

Becoming an author

In this chapter we've explored ways to get your message out there. I cannot end this section without mentioning the power of writing your own book. I've shied away from discussing this until now as this is my very first book, so the old *Imposter Syndrome* is rearing its ugly head and saying: 'Who are you to tell others to write a book when yours isn't published yet?' But by the time you read this, I will of course be in print! Becoming an author gives you the ultimate authority (it's even written in the word). Not ready to write your own book yet? Consider finding a co-authored book to contribute to as a way to get you started. A book gives you a way to get your message out there loud and clear and is a brilliant marketing tool. A book allows you to bring people into your way of thinking without huge financial investment. A book enables you to build trust, loyalty and referrals. What can I say? It has taken me several years to get this one down on paper, and sometimes timing places a crucial part. To get your book out into the world consider traditional publishing, self-publishing and hybrid publishing. Whichever way you choose to do it, there's no bigger statement about who you are and what you do than your own words in a book.

In each of the areas I have covered in this chapter - awards, podcasts, speaking, webinars, books - there is a word of caution I wish to share with you. Whatever you put out into the world, make sure it is something you want to be known for, something you are proud to be the expert in. Of course, it is more than OK to evolve, develop and pivot in your business and personal interests, but check in with yourself that you are actually self-labelling as an expert in the right thing.

When I launched my online business and speaking career, I focused on Mums and how they can get ready to move on with their own passions. One of my skillsets is mindfulness. Soon, I was being asked to speak on mindfulness, write articles on mindfulness and be interviewed on mindfulness. It was not the direction I wanted to go in. It was the same with the 'Mum' space. I grew out of it. I stepped away from opportunities that were taking me off course. It wasn't always easy to do, but I am glad I did.

What do you want to be known for, to be visible for? Choose the right path and go at it hard. Get visible for what you really want to be associated with.

10

EPILOGUE

On the other side of Visibility.

On the other side of your fears around visibility lie the rewards you deserve - increased credibility, increased income, increased connections, referrals and opportunities. The hard truth is that nobody will cross those troubled waters for you. Only you can take the action to get out there and be seen. I used to blame everyone around me for my lack of success. I'd complain about the unfairness of my industry, that I wasn't wealthy enough to have connections, that I wasn't born into the right family, that my face didn't fit. I even told myself that there was something wrong with me, that I pushed people away because either I wasn't good enough or because I was a threat. All whilst knowing that I *was* talented, capable, able, good enough. The work I did around my limiting beliefs changed everything. I realised that my own thoughts and blocks had kept me from building connections. I realised that elements of my body language belied my otherwise confident exterior. I understood that choosing where to belong and focusing on finding the doors to open rather than the ones that were shut would transform my professional success. With new knowledge on how fearful I had been about stepping into the spotlight (whilst craving it) I could go at my life with a sense of adventure rather than risk. I could be playful in who I approached. I could view possibility where before I had seen danger. This shift in the way I think has catapulted me into new directions and now I can achieve whatever I put my mind to, without fear of failure. I won't pretend that everything I do now works out brilliantly first time. It doesn't. But I have learned to treat failure as an exciting, often vital stepping stone on the path to where I want to be. I don't waste much time, energy or attention on failure. If I ever do, I catch myself and my thoughts and language and make immediate steps to focus on empowering language.

In this book I've shared how you can transform how you think about yourself and your place in your industry. I have shared my steps to achieve visibility and I've given you the know-how to build your own visibility strategy. I believe that what we believe, we can achieve. What we tell our mind, what we remind our mind and what we take strides towards can become our reality - perhaps not straightaway, and not always in exactly the way we planned, but consistent action towards visibility reaps rewards.

Holding on to the big vision in your mind of the grandest version of your dream will help you get there. Visualisation is a powerful tool that works - Olympic athletes use it in their mental training. Leading CEO's use the technique to sharpen their leadership abilities. Coaches understand that reliving the end goal of success over and over helps the mind to combat challenges. It is easier to achieve what the mind has already programmed itself for.

To accompany this book, I am gifting you a free guided visualisation for confidence. All you have to do is visit my website to download it. It helps train your brain to remember how it feels to be confident, to be *enough* and to ignite and deepen neural pathways that enable more confident behaviours and actions. You can download it at www.annaparkernaples.co.uk/confidence-audio.

Take action to become super-clear on where you are going, on the dream you hold for yourself. Planning ahead is easier once you have established that picture of what you really want to achieve on its grandest scale.

Activity: The dream

Describe your big business dream:

The service I provide is:

I help people to:

I describe myself and my work in the following way:

If I allow myself to be visible, and charge what I am worth, financially it would mean:

Within five years from now, if I were to have created my dream and fulfilled my potential, my life would look, feel and sound like: (Describe this in as much detail as possible.)

What do I need to do within one year from now to be on target for my dream?

In three months from now?

In one month?

Today?

What action can you take *right now* to set you on the path to fulfilling your potential?

Once you have completed this step, take immediate action to get the ball rolling. Send that email, do that research, make that call. DO SOMETHING to start that new trajectory towards getting visible.

Final Note

I hope that this book has encouraged you to step up and be seen. I cannot wait to hear about the ways you have challenged yourself to **get visible** and the impact it has on your life.

It's your time.

Be seen, be heard, be remembered.

'Anything's possible when you get visible.'

Much love

Anna x

ABOUT THE AUTHOR

Anna Parker-Naples is a multi-award-winning entrepreneur, business coach and host of Entrepreneurs Get Visible podcast (reaching no.1 in the iTunes charts internationally, outranking the likes of Tony Robbins, Marie Forleo, Amy Porterfield and Gary Vaynerchuk).

She lives in Bedfordshire with her husband, three children, her dog Oscar…the family cat, and two hamsters. Anna was told in 2010 that she may never walk again due to a complication in pregnancy. Through NLP (Neuro Linguistic Programming) and mindset work, she transformed her physical health, fully recovered and embraced a journey of adventure and discovery to become the successful performer she had always dreamed she would become.

After landing herself on the red carpets in Hollywood as a celebrated Voice Actor, Anna changed focus, and now uses her skills and experience to help other entrepreneurs and creatives have the courage and strategy to become the go-to expert in their field.

Anna has spoken on the same stages as celebrities such as Will Young & Ruby Wax and won an international award for her work to inspire others alongside Rio Ferdinand and singing sensation Adele. She has been featured in Metro, Psychologies, BBC Radio, iNews, Health & Wellness and Thrive Global. Anna regularly gives keynote speeches about visibility, imposter syndrome and podcasting for authority.

Since publishing the first edition of the no. 1 bestseller *Get Visible*, Anna has established The Podcast Membership and is CEO of her own Podcast Production Agency offering launch consultancy and full production services. She has been responsible for 100+ podcasts launching globally, achieving chart-topping success for her clients. Her second book *Podcast with Impact: How to Start & Launch Your Podcast Properly* is now available. Anna works with purpose-driven entrepreneurs to create effective online businesses through her high-level mentoring and mastermind programs.

'Anything's possible when you get visible.'

Find out more about Anna

Website: www.annaparkernaples.com
Facebook Page:
www.facebook.com/AnnaParkerNaplesCoach
Facebook Group:
www.facebook.com/groups/EntrepreneursGetVisible
Resources and Free Downloads:
Social Media Visibility Checklist:
www.annaparkernaples.co.uk/social-media-checklist
Launch Your Podcast Checklist
www.annaparkernaples.co.uk/podcastchecklist
Money Making Mindset Audio:
www.annaparkernaples.co.uk/money-making-audio
Confidence Visualisation:
www.annaparkernaples.co.uk/confidence-audio
The Podcast Membership:
www.ThePodcastMembership.com
Podcast Production and Consultancy:
www.annaparkernaples.co.uk/podcast-production

 facebook.com/AnnaParkerNaplesCoach

 twitter.com/annaparkernaple

 instagram.com/annaparkernaples

 linkedin.com/in/annaparkernaples

Lightning Source UK Ltd.
Milton Keynes UK
UKHW020009020721
386482UK00002B/26/J